Reflections on Aging and Spiritual Growth

D0965256

Reflections on Aging and Spiritual Growth

Andrew J. Weaver
Harold G. Koenig
Phyllis C. Roe

Abingdon Press
Nashville

REFLECTIONS ON AGING AND SPIRITUAL GROWTH

This book is printed on recycled, acid-free, elemental-chlorine–free paper.

Library of Congress Cataloging-in-Publication Data

Reflections on aging and spiritual growth / [edited by] Andrew J.
Weaver, Harold G. Koenig, Phyllis C. Roe.
    p.   cm.
    Includes bibliographical references.
    ISBN 0-687-09519-0 (alk. paper)
    1. Aged—Religious life. 2. Aging—Religious aspects—
Christianity. I. Weaver, Andrew J., 1947–   . II. Koenig, Harold
George. III. Roe, Phyllis C., 1947– .
BV4580.R44 1998
248.8'5—dc21   98-21604
                                                    CIP

Scripture quotations, unless otherwise indicated, are from the New Revised Standard Version Bible, copyright © 1989, by the Division of Christian Education of the National Council of the Churches of Christ in the United States of America.

Scripture quotations noted RSV are from the Revised Standard Version of the Bible, copyright 1946, 1952, 1971 by the Division of Christian Education of the National Council of the Churches of Christ in the USA. Used by permission.

"It's a Sweet Life," by Kathleen Norris, is reprinted from her book *The Cloister Walk* (New York: Riverhead Books, 1996).

98   99   00   01   02   03   04   05   06   07 — 10   9   8   7   6   5   4   3   2   1

MANUFACTURED IN THE UNITED STATES OF AMERICA

To my maternal grandmother,

SARAH HATTIE ALLEN HAM,

who imparted to me a longing for God—AJW

To my

PARENTS,

who have been a blessing from God—HGK

To my

OLDER FRIENDS,

from whom I've learned that life can be good at any age—PCR

CONTENTS

ACKNOWLEDGMENTS

I am very grateful to the Reverend Carolyn L. Stapleton and Donalyn K. Keli'ipule'ole for their invaluable help while I completed this project.

I am thankful to the late Father Henri Nouwen, who inspired the vision of this book through his remarkable writings, including *Aging: The Fulfillment of Life*.

I am thankful to the late Senator Terry Sanford for writing the foreword for this volume. As Governor of and Senator from North Carolina he led a life marked by taking the road less traveled. He loved justice, did mercy, and walked humbly with God, and we all have been the better for it, most especially the daughters and sons of the South.—AJW

CONTRIBUTORS

Roberta C. Bondi earned the Doctor of Philosophy degree at Oxford University and is Professor of Church History, Candler School of Theology, Emory University, Atlanta, Georgia. She is the author of *To Love as God Loves, To Pray and to Love, Memories of God, In Ordinary Time,* and *A Place to Pray.*

Monica Furlong is an author and member of the Church of England who lives in London. She has written numerous books: *Merton: A Biography; Travelling In; Wise Child; Juniper; Zen Effects: The Life of Alan Watts; Visions and Longing: Medieval Women Mystics; Emma Lazarus: Poet of Jewish People; Therese of Lisieux; The Wisdom of Julian of Norwich; Contemplation Now; A Dangerous Delight: Women and Power in the Church.*

James A. Harnish is the Senior Pastor of Hyde Park United Methodist Church, Tampa, Florida. A graduate of Asbury Theological Seminary, he has served for twenty-five years as a pastor in Florida. He and his wife, Marsha, have two "Generation X" daughters. He has written six books on spiritual growth, including *Men at Midlife: Steering Through the Detours, God Isn't Finished With Us Yet,* and *Believe in Me.*

Harold G. Koenig is board certified in geriatric psychiatry and geriatric medicine, currently serving on the faculty at Duke as Associate Professor of Psychiatry and Assistant Professor of Medicine. He is founder and Director of the Center for the Study of Religion/Spirituality and Health at Duke and has written more than 120 scientific articles and book chapters. He has authored or coauthored seven books, including *Aging and God, Is Religion Good for Your Health?* and *Counseling Troubled Older Adults: A Handbook for Pastors and Religious Caregivers* with Andrew J. Weaver.

Clarence Liu is an Asian American writer and hospital ministry coordinator for Interfaith Ministries of Hawaii at the Hawaii State Hospital. He has led retreats in Asia and the United States, drawing from his experiences in Zen practice and Centering Prayer. He resides in Honolulu with his wife, Pat Novak Liu.

Kathleen Norris is the author of three books of nonfiction: *Dakota: A Spiritual Geography; The Cloister Walk;* and *Amazing Grace: A Vocabulary of Faith.* Her most recent book of poems is *Little Girls in Church.* A recipient of grants from the Bush and Guggenheim foundations, she has been in residence twice at the Institute for Ecumenical and Cultural Research at St. John's Abbey in Collegeville, Minnesota. She lives in South Dakota and has been, for over twelve years, an oblate of Assumption Abbey in North Dakota.

M. Basil Pennington, O.C.S.O, is a Cistercian monk of the Abbey of Our Lady of St. Joseph, in Spencer, Massachusetts, currently residing in Our Lady of Joy Monastery, Hong Kong. He has written numerous books including *Awake in the Spirit: A Personal Handbook; Bernard of Clairvaux: A Lover Teaching the Way of Love; Call to the Center: The Gospel's Invitation to Deeper Prayer; On Retreat with Thomas Merton; Light from the Cloister; The Monastic Way; Thomas Merton Brother Monk: The Quest for True Freedom; Vatican II: We've Only Just Begun; Daily We Touch Him: Practical Religious Experiences; Lessons from the Monastery That Touch Your Life; Praying by Hand: Rediscovering the Rosary as a Way of Prayer.*

Phyllis C. Roe is an ordained United Methodist minister, a fellow with the American Association of Pastoral Counselors, and the Executive Director of the Samaritan Counseling Center of

Hawaii in Honolulu. She holds a Doctor of Theology degree from Emory University, Atlanta, Georgia. She was formerly on the senior staff of the Georgia Association for Pastoral Care in Atlanta and served as Director of Supervised Ministry on the faculty of Candler School of Theology, Emory University. She has written articles and book reviews for professional journals.

Donald J. Shelby has been the Senior Pastor of First United Methodist Church in Santa Monica, California, for twenty-three years. He is a graduate of the School of Theology at Claremont and has written *The Unsettling Season, Bold Expectations, Forever Beginning, Meeting the Messiah.* He and his spouse, Jean, have two daughters, two sons-in-law, and three grandchildren.

Orlo C. Strunk, Jr. is Emeritus Professor from Boston University in Pastoral Care. He is a pastoral psychotherapist at the Samaritan Counseling Center in Myrtle Beach, South Carolina, and the managing editor of the *Journal of Pastoral Care.* His books include *Privacy, Experience, Understanding and Expression; The Psychology of Religion: Historical and Interpretative Readings;* and *The Secret Self.*

Gene M. Tucker is Professor of Old Testament, Emeritus, at Candler School of Theology, Emory University, where he was on the faculty for twenty-five years. He was educated at McMurry College and Yale University. He has been active in the Society of Biblical Literature, having served as its president in 1996. He is a United Methodist minister and served as a member of the committee that translated the NRSV. He is the author, coauthor, or editor of seventeen books, including *Form Criticism of the Old Testament* and (with Fred B. Craddock, John H. Hayes, and Carl R. Holladay) *Preaching Through the Christian Year* (three volumes). His present projects include the commentary on Isaiah 1–39 for the *New Interpreter's Bible.*

Jane E. Vennard, ordained by the United Church of Christ, is a spiritual director, retreat leader, workshop leader, and lecturer.

She is adjunct faculty at Iliff School of Theology in Denver, Colorado, where she teaches courses on prayer and spirituality. She is the author of *Praying for Friends and Enemies* and *Praying with Body and Soul.*

Andrew J. Weaver is a United Methodist minister and psychologist who works at Hawaii State Hospital in Kaneohe. Licensed as both a clinical psychologist and a marriage and family therapist, he is on the clinical faculty of the University of Hawaii's department of psychology. He is a graduate of Perkins School of Theology, Southern Methodist University in Dallas, Texas, and the Wright Institute Graduate School of Clinical Psychology in Berkeley, California. He has written over fifty articles and book chapters on the role of clergy in mental health care. He recently coauthored *Counseling Troubled Older Adults: A Handbook for Pastors and Religious Caregivers* with Harold G. Koenig.

William H. Willimon is Dean of the Chapel and Professor of Christian Ministry at Duke University where he directs the programs of campus ministry and teaches in the Divinity and Undergraduate schools. He is the author of more than forty books, including (with Thomas H. Naylor) *The Search for Meaning, The Abandoned Generation: Rethinking Higher Education,* and *Downsizing the USA.* He has earned degrees from Wofford College, Yale University, and Emory University, and been awarded honorary degrees from six colleges and universities. The Willimons have two young adult children, both of whom are students at Wofford College.

FOREWORD

I became interested in aging, as I like to say, when aging got interested in me. I examined nearly three hundred books and documents and in time wrote a little book on aging *(Outlive Your Enemies)* in good health, based on the medical and scientific information available.

I found four rules that targeted physical conditioning, medical precautions, proper eating, and dropping bad habits such as smoking and couch potatoing. I neglected the most important element of successful aging, which transcends strong muscles and good digestion and regular medical examinations. I did not emphasize the spirituality that both comforts and promotes graceful aging.

True, I talked about good deeds and concern for others and jettisoning grudges and bitterness and hate. I talked about the acceptance of death, expressed by one of my book characters.

> I could have been killed in the war, or by chance on the highway, or by some eager illness. I was preparing for a chance death, by getting enough insurance to protect my family. Now it is no longer chance I am facing. It is certainty. Even if I am lucky, death is out there waiting. I can accept it calmly. It is not beyond the horizon—we can look at it. What is my image of death? It could be a vicious black bear with great claws and jaws, but for me it is a loving shepherd ready to embrace me and warm me, a shivering child, within the folds of his cloak.

The essays in this volume get at the essence and the fulfillment of a long life, the satisfaction that comes from acknowledging the power of God from contriteness for transgressions, from the forgiveness sought and granted. Aging presents the chance to set things aright, for making peace with your Maker as teenagers make peace with their parents.

I am not suggesting that these essays have neglected the worldly aspects, the science of aging, the mental health needs. Quite the contrary. But in addition, they comprehend that stress that damages and shortens so many lives can be and is reduced and eliminated by the spiritual influence of one's religion.

Life must have meaning for an individual from the very beginning of comprehension, and appreciating and intensifying meaning, without doubt, affects health and longevity. It is doubtful that meaning in one's life can be understood, enhanced, and accepted without the strength of a spirituality and faith.

It is tempting now for me to review each article, to suggest the excitement and promise that each holds, but that is not the purpose of my brief entry into the pages of this book. Our writers bring a wide view to the opportunities and joys, as well as the perils of growing older, and help us find the compassion for all and the acceptance of what must be.

To read this book is as if we were privileged to sit in a retreat for several days with these thoughtful women and men, discovering the fulfillment of life, its purpose and meanings, in a conference room atop a mountain, viewing in one direction the moving, rising, falling tides of the tumultuous ocean, and in the other direction the placid, broad, shining lake with a scattering of sailboats running with a gentle breeze into the evening sun.

You will enjoy your conversation with these people.

Terry Sanford
President Emeritus of Duke University,
Former U.S. Senator and Governor of North Carolina
November 1997

Introduction

REFLECTIONS ON AGING— What Does Science Say?

ANDREW J. WEAVER AND HAROLD G. KOENIG

Even to your old age I am [God], and to gray hairs I will carry you.
—Isaiah 46:4 RSV

As we age what is the place of religion and spirituality in our lives? Is spirituality helpful or harmful to our health? Does our faith help make us whole as we move into our later years? The relevance of these questions for the church is obvious when we look at a few statistics. About one in eight Americans is currently sixty-five years of age or over, a figure that will increase to about one in five by 2030.[1] The membership of churches is aging even more rapidly than the general population. Eighty percent of older Americans attend worship services weekly. By the year 2000, almost half of mainline Protestants will be over age sixty.[2] The mental health needs of older persons are increasingly becoming the central counseling concern for pastors.[3]

One of the most important (and often unrecognized) facts in modern science is that research has shown consistently that nurturing, nonpunitive religion is good for your mental and physical health. Over the past three decades numerous researchers have found strong relationships between traditional Christian practices (such as regular worship attendance, Scripture reading, prayer) and positive mental and physical health among seniors.

Religiously involved older adults are generally less prone to suicide, depression, anxiety, and alcoholism and are more satisfied with their lives and have a greater sense of well-being. Studies have found that older adults who practice their faith regularly even have lower blood pressure, fewer heart attacks, stronger immune systems to fight diseases such as cancer, and are less likely to die of coronary artery disease.[4]

Aging involves increasing numbers of losses and other psychological stressors. The negative effects of stress play a significant role in many psychosomatic illnesses like stomach ulcers, high blood pressure, stroke and heart attacks. One-fourth to one-third of older adults find religion to be the most important factor that enables them to cope with high stress, including chronic illness.[5] By reducing stress and providing life with meaning and purpose, faith practices can prevent emotional and psychosomatic illnesses. This is even more true for older women and African-Americans, over half of whom may use religion as a coping behavior during times of stress.[6,7] Faith commitment can serve as a buffer against hardships, diminish loneliness, and encourage hopefulness. It offers an active support system and provides the opportunities for meaningful volunteer work. Studies tell us that helping others is an excellent way to gain fulfillment and greater life satisfaction.[8]

Research also shows that religious commitment can change over time. Sixty percent of older persons report that they have become more devout with age, while only 5 percent indicate that religion's importance has decreased. While religious conversion usually has been considered a phenomenon of the young, a revealing pattern emerges when older adults are asked about changes in their faith. In a study of 850 hospitalized men age sixty-five or older, one-third reported having had a religious experience that changed their lives; 42 percent experienced this change after the age of fifty. It is quite common for persons in their seventies and eighties to experience a change in feelings about religion, particularly when faced with physical illness and disability.[9] These research findings indicate that religious experience is not static but dynamic among seniors and often increases in significance during the later years.

Let us not forget, however, that many older adults with a very strong and abiding faith in God experience both physical and mental illness. As the Scriptures remind us, God "sends rain on the righteous and on the unrighteous" (Matthew 5:45). One cannot conclude that those without illnesses have less faith or are less faithful than those with difficulties. However, studies have shown that even if depressed, those with faith in God recover from their depression faster than those without such faith, and this is especially true for older adults who are both depressed and severely disabled.[10] It is during the most difficult times in life that people need their religious faith to give them hope and endurance, and to motivate them toward recovery. Religious beliefs and spiritual practices, then, help prevent the onset of emotional problems as well as speed their healing when they do occur.

Reflections on Aging and Spiritual Growth gives creative, experienced voices in the Christian community an opportunity to reflect on aging as a part of their faith journey and share with us their insights. These authors offer lessons and wisdom about the changes and challenges of aging. How have their losses deepened or diminished faith? How does one affirm aging as a person of faith in a society perpetually fascinated with the novel and young? What spiritual direction might be offered to others on the journey of faith, young or old? What counsel does our Christian heritage offer us as we live in or approach our later years? The writers represent many areas of service within the life of the faith community: laity, pastors, chaplains, pastoral counselors, scholars, monastics, and spiritual directors. Collectively, they have more than eight hundred years of experience in the faith journey. Their insights can help us to more fully understand and to appreciate the often hidden scientific fact that good health and healthy spirituality go hand in hand as we grow older.

Notes

1. M. Dean, "Grey growth," *Lancet*, 335(1990), 1330-31.
2. G. H. Gallup, *Religion in America: 1994, Supplement* (Princeton, N.J.: The Gallup Poll, 1994).
3. H. G. Koenig and A. J. Weaver, *Counseling Troubled Older Adults: A Handbook for Clergy and Other Religious Caregivers* (Nashville: Abingdon Press, 1997).
4. H. G. Koenig, *Is Religion Good for Your Health? The Effects of Religion on Physical and Mental Health* (New York: Haworth Press, 1997).
5. H. G. Koenig, *Research in Religion and Aging* (Westport, Conn.: Greenwood Press, 1995).
6. H. G. Koenig, L. K. George, and I. C. Siegler, "The use of religion and other emotion-regulating coping strategies among adults," *The Gerontologist*, 28 (3), 303-10.
7. N. Krause and T. V. Van Tran, "Stress and religious involvement among older Blacks," *Journal of Gerontology*, 44 (1989), S4-S13.
8. N. Krause, A. R. Herzog, and E. Baker, "Providing support to others and well-being in later life," *Journal of Gerontology*, 47 (1992), P300-P311.
9. H. G. Koenig, H. J. Cohen, D. G. Blazer, C. Pieper, K. G. Meador, F. Shelp, V. Goli, and B. DiPasquale, "Religious coping and depression among elderly, hospitalized medically ill men," *American Journal of Psychiatry*, 149 (12), 1693-1700.
19. Ibid.

1

※

SMOKE, TEARS, AND FIRE: SPIRITUALITY AND AGING

※

ROBERTA C. BONDI

W hen I was a child of eight or ten, I couldn't imagine myself getting old; in fact, I couldn't picture myself growing up at all. It is strange to remember this now, considering that I was such a daydreamer and a reader. My religious life was certainly imaginative. God and the idea of Jesus dying on a cross because of my sins terrified me even more than the minister and the well-dressed Sunday school teacher who taught us Bible stories. Regular visits to my Kentucky grandmother's Pond Fork Baptist Church summer revivals also found fertile ground in me. I was so impressed by the images of the Second Coming and the Last Judgment I encountered there that I would lie in bed at night for months afterward, sleepless and terrified, unable to escape those images.

Certainly, my imagination was active enough in every area of my life. Without any effort I experienced what I imagined to be the feelings of the lonely rock I tripped over when I went out to play by myself in the skimpy brown grass outside our New York garden apartment. Susan Cagle, my best friend from next door, and I pretended endlessly we were dogs and cats; I spent hours on my hands and knees meowing and purring as Susan panted, barked, and whined. Floating like a ballet dancer, dying, living underground in a secret cave, riding on the sleigh with the Snow Queen, having a room I didn't share with my little brother, spending eternity in hell, putting my face against the black and white fur of the panda in the Bronx Zoo—none of these were too much for me. But imagining myself actually being twenty-five years old, an ordinary, powerful, confident, self-sufficient, outgoing, competent grown-up who actually talked to other grownups? That was beyond my powers.

Whether I could imagine it at ten or not, I did grow up, and in my twenties I was astounded, first, that it happened at all, and second, that being grown up was so unlike anything I would ever have expected. By the time I was twenty-five I had been married nearly seven years, but I was still a student. I didn't feel powerful; in fact, I hardly felt in control of my life at all. Whether I was pleasing my husband caused me great anxiety. I worried constantly about meeting other people's expectations and I sought their approval compulsively. I rarely experienced myself as competent. I continued to suffer from shyness as well as the dependent loneliness of childhood, and trying to talk to adults even a little older than I was excruciating.

Still, being twenty-five was much better than being ten. I knew this was true not just from experience, but also because I read it in the papers and the magazines, and I took seriously the things they said: at twenty-five a woman was in the prime of her life. I was in my best years, and I ought to enjoy it. I had the privileges of adulthood at the same time I had my youth, and youth was a commodity everybody wanted, particularly women who needed to please men (all of us, in those days, who were not in convents). There was a lot to be said for my life at twenty-five. That was the year I went to England to begin my graduate work. It was the era of the Beatles and the miniskirt, and in spite of all the difficulties I've just listed, and some others besides, I loved my years there.

During my twenties, for the first time I found it easy to imagine myself aging. Why not? What I read told me what it would be like. As a fifty-year-old woman I would be "over the hill." No matter what was going on inside me, having lost my youthful looks and my usefulness, I could expect to be a person of no interest or significance to anyone. No one would want to know what I thought about anything. I would no longer be able to wear bright colors or silly clothes. I would have no sense of humor. I would be politically conservative in such a way that I would believe I was entitled to everything I had, and I would join the women's society in church, where I would spend a lot of time deploring the lax morality of the younger generation and talking about the will of God.

Needless to say, if this dreary business is what I expected my aging would be about, I certainly didn't expect much for my ongoing spiritual life. Religion, as it both attracted and repelled me throughout my childhood and early adult years, had always been a painful business. The only God I knew was the judgmental God of my childhood to whom I related exclusively in terms of sin and forgiveness. I longed for this God to love me, but flawed as I knew I was, I didn't believe I was worthy of that love. All I wanted was to escape God, preferably by forgetting everything I knew about God. That I might come later in my life to know God in a different way or relate to God in other, truly life-giving, terms never occurred to me.

How different the ongoing process of adult life has been from anything I ever imagined! There is very little resemblance, spiritually and every other way, between actually being in my fifties and what I thought it would be like when I was twenty-five. I was so frightened, so wounded and in need of approval, so despairing that the things that caused me pain could ever begin to be healed! It would have seemed impossible then that I should look back over my life from where I am now and not only know that it is a good thing to be fifty-five, but also be glad that there is no one on earth whose life I would trade for mine.

What has made aging so different from and so much more wonderful than I thought it would be? A lot of it is circumstantial: I am blessed with children, a mother, friends, and students whom I both love and enjoy, and who love and enjoy me in return. I have an exceptional husband who is my companion in every way, one who, when I complain about my spreading body, tells me that he is glad that I have at last come into my mature shape. I am in fairly good health.

I have also been blessed by the women's movement, which really took hold in my thirties (the decade of the seventies). Having benefited from the fact that women have far more opportunities outside the home than they had thirty years ago, I have work that I value. At the same time, like so many other women older and younger than I, I have been given the tools to help me reject a large number of the earlier cultural stereotypes about women—their looks, brains, and emotions—that hurt me and made me feel helpless in my younger years.

What has made it possible for me to come to where I am now, however, is something over and above any of this, something I only had glimpses of in my twenties: it is a knowledge of my own grounding in God, who over the years has slowly, steadily freed me from both debilitating perfectionism and guilt, and from the energy-sapping burden of trying to please everybody I know in both my personal and professional lives. This grounding in God continues to give me the strength to discern, work, and suffer for what I myself value. At the same time, it has increasingly allowed me a space to confront and be confronted by my own wounds to my ability to love and receive love and to seek healing from God.

I didn't come to this sense of grounding on my own; rather, most of it has come as I have meditated on and wrestled in prayer with the words of the fourth-, fifth-, and sixth-century Christian teachers I study and teach my own students in seminary. From these teachers I have most fundamentally learned that whatever our culture tells us about life being an inevitably demoralizing business of falling apart, it is not what human life is about. Bodies do wear out and our minds do get slower, but human beings are made in the image of God who is love; and God's intention for us, if we choose to pursue it, is continual growth—growth in love both of God and neighbor. This growth, if we choose it, will go on not only in our own lifetime but throughout eternity itself.[1]

This vision of human life has been freeing and encouraging to me as I have grown older in all sorts of ways. One of the most important is this: From the time I was a child I had accepted the idea that from the day I became a Christian I ought to be able to love the Lord my God with all my heart and my neighbor as myself. Having always been aware that I didn't love in this way, I had also always felt like a failure. To hear my ancient Christian teachers tell me repeatedly that I should expect, rather, that love both of God and of other people is something to be learned over a lifetime has little by little set me free. It has given me back the energy that was previously consumed in trying to survive my own sense of guilt and failure so that I could actually do the internal and external work of finding healing for the wounds that would keep me from love. I had also accepted what most of us have heard from childhood, namely, that a faithful person faces all difficulties in a state of peace because she has "turned everything over to the Lord." Knowing that even as a little girl I had never had "peace" in this sense as I struggled painfully against anger, depression, and grief, I had despaired of ever being a "real Christian." My ancient teachers have helped me put this destructively enslaving myth to rest. Far from expecting peace, Amma Syncletica, whose words are included in an early collection of the teachings of the fathers and mothers of the Egyptian desert,[2] is recorded as describing the process of the Christian life in this way:

> In the beginning there are a great many battles and a good deal of suffering for those who are advancing towards God, and afterwards, ineffable joy. It is like those who wish to light a fire; at first they are choked by the smoke and cry, and by this means obtain what they seek. So we must also kindle the divine fire in ourselves through tears and hard work.[3]

When I look back over the tears and hard work I have expended over the years, what I see now is not a mark of my failures, or, for that matter, a tragedy that I should have suffered in the ways I have, but simply a necessary part of the journey toward the healing of love that every Christian must make. My teachers also taught me about the importance of regular prayer as a major place I could do the different kinds of work of growing in love over the years. Like so many of us, I grew up with my images of God and of my loving but perfectionistic, judgmental father so mixed together that I could not trust God, much less love God. The long-term practice of prayer, including learning to risk being who I really am in God's presence and learning to confront God, has allowed me to find out firsthand that not only is God trustworthy and lovable, but that God both loves and likes me in return. It is this knowledge that has allowed me to face and seek God's help for the things in myself, memories, hurtful dispositions, and wounded ways of being that have needed healing.

Finally, my teachers have helped me and continue to help me focus on what is most important to me as I grow older. Abba Anthony used to say: "Whoever hammers a lump of iron, first decides what he is going to make of it, a scythe, a sword, or an axe. Even so we ought to make up our minds what kind of virtue we want to forge or we labour in vain."[4] I am not talking here about obsessively trying to shape my own personality. I am referring to the fact that I need to continue to have long-term goals and priorities in my spiritual life. Abba Ammonas said, "I have spent fourteen years in Scetis asking God night and day to grant me the victory over anger."[5] By this he as well as Anthony remind me that I should not expect that my own internal impatience with others, irritability, and tendencies toward despair will go away easily by themselves; I must work at them. At the same time, they have kept me in mind of the fact that I must also not expect to be able to do the work of writing and teaching I am called to do unless I discipline myself by setting priorities in the use of my time.

As Amma Syncletica would tell me with her fire metaphor, this discipline to remain focused has become increasingly easy for me as I've gotten older. Whether this will continue to be true in another fifteen or twenty years, however, I cannot say. From what I read, true old age is very different from what I am experiencing now. I am not looking forward to losing physical strength, nor having the people I love die. Still, none of the gifts that have come to me as I have aged have been imaginable to me in advance. As little as I may know what is ahead of me, I am able to believe from my own experience what my ancient teachers have been telling me all these years: love in God, in whatever form it takes, is a continual growth in love that never comes to an end.

Notes

1. Cf. Gregory of Nyssa, "On Perfection" and "On the Christian Mode of Life," in *Gregory of Nyssa: Ascetical Writings*, ed. and trans. Virginia Woods Callahan, Fathers of the Church, vol. 58 (Washington, D.C.: Catholic University of America, 1967).
2. The words of three women teachers are included in this collection, those of Syncletica, Sara, and Theodora. The collection itself is in English translation, *The Sayings of the Desert Fathers: The Alphabetical Collection*, trans. Benedicta Ward SLG, Cistercian Publications, 1984. For a modern encounter with more of what these ancient teachers have to say see my *To Love as God Loves: Conversations with the Early Church* and *To Pray and to Love: Conversations on Prayer with the Early Church*, both published by Augsburg-Fortress Press.
3. Syncletica 1, Ward, pp. 230-31.
4. Anthony 35, Ward, p. 8.
5. Ammonas 3, Ward, p. 26.

2

LONG ON THE JOURNEY

M. BASIL PENNINGTON

About ten years ago I wrote a little book entitled *Long on the Journey*. Since then I have been longer on the journey. I have had more experience and I hope more insight. This month I began to collect Social Security and Medicare. Getting up and down is a little more difficult than it used to be. I find myself a bit breathless at the top of the stairs. The knees ache. I have to watch what I eat. I seem to spend more time going to "specialists." The hearing isn't what it used to be, and I won't be able to wear contact lenses much longer.

Of course, all of this could absorb more and more of my attention. But that would be my choice. And my choice certainly is not to let my life close in on my woes. There is too much out there, too much that is wonderful, beautiful, exciting. And there is too much that is wondrous in there, in the kingdom that is within, to let my time and attention be absorbed by such an uninteresting, if not depressing, subject as the woes of getting old.

The Gift of Time

One of the graces of growing old is the gift of time. As responsibilities fall away and friends pass on, there is more and more liberated time. Again, there is a choice, a freedom to decide what to do with this time. The years go on, the diminishments increase. More and more things have to be let go. Not because of any lack of interest: the energy just isn't there. More and more we prize the quiet hours in that favorite chair, perhaps one that is blessed with a special view from the window or a special array of pictures that keep loved ones near.

Most precious are those hours or minutes spent sitting in that chair with a friend close by. How wonderful it is to grow old together! Unfortunately, this is the privilege of a relative few. And the friends who come to sit and share the quiet hours become fewer and fewer. There is more and more space to fill.

For me, the quiet hours in my recliner have indeed become more and more precious. I look forward to them and look forward to the time when I will have more of them. Why is this?

Well, for one thing, they are filled with friends and friendship. Sometimes they do afford me the time to really just enjoy a friend, waste time with the friend, with no sense of something waiting to be done, of a certain restrictive *limit to* the time we can enjoy together. I sense this is a bit of a beginning of the joy of eternal life, just being with friends with nothing else to do.

Of course, much of the time there is no friend there—in the flesh. But so present is the spirit, in the reality of memory, in the books of pictures I take out and leaf through. We are together again in wonderful moments of life. And they can be savored now in a way that they could not be when they were rushing by in the midst of so many doings. Yes, there are the painful, the sad, the sorrowful memories. But I have the right to choose. I can "flip the channel" and dwell with the memories of my choice, although at times it is consoling to hold again some painful moments, to hold them before God in healing and prayerful love.

To Be with Our Friend

Here is my greatest joy: to be with my Friend of friends, to have the time to waste together. I see God in all the wonders of the creation about me. We enjoy walks together. Or just looking out the window together. Or looking at those pictures or walking down memory lane. Every love and concern, every joy and sorrow of mine is shared. And now I have the time to experience that. And with my Friend to touch and to heal, or to laugh again and know the warmth of love.

At times I let him talk to me. I take my Bible down from the little shrine in my room. I like to keep the Bible enthroned, for I know God is present in a special way in this living word. As I hold this old "friend"—the Bible in my shrine was given to me many years ago by two very dear friends, a gay couple who radiated Christ and his love and care—I am deeply aware of the presence of my Friend in the Word. I ask the Holy Spirit, God's Spirit of love who has been poured out in my heart and who inspired the writers of these pages, to make them now a living communication to me from my Beloved. Then I listen, to hear what my Friend has to say to me today.

I listen and hear what the Lord says to me today. It is wondrous how familiar words, in the context of this day, can say something wholly new. Sometimes it is the familiar, comforting, reassuring, or challenging message that is heard again. Whatever it is, God and I are soon in conversation. There is no rush. No place to go. We can, and we often do, spend a half-hour, an hour or more, on a single sentence, a phrase or word.

When it is time to bestir myself, there is in my heart a tremendous sense of gratitude. How good is my God to come and sit with me, to talk to me so intimately. I thank him. And there is a new word inscribed in my heart, to remain vividly there as I move on. Sometimes to remain there for life, it seems. I can even now recall words we shared years and years ago. And there are the words we shared last week. And there is today's: *Repent, for the kingdom of God is here.* "Repent" brings to mind the Latin *re* and *petere* = to seek again. The Lord invites me to turn back to him, to seek him again with all my heart, for he is in my heart: the Kingdom of God is within, it is here. What joy, what peace I can find when I let all that babble of thoughts and cares and worries go and just seek him within.

Sometimes that is how my time of talking with the Lord with the Bible in hand ends. I just let the Bible go and rest within.

Sometimes when I sit down I don't want to take up the Bible. I just want to sit and be—be with him who is within. Nothing needs to be said. Or at most, a single, simple little word of love that allows us to be together.

Some might call this contemplative prayer—and I believe it is. But I think I first learned it many, many years ago, the summer I was four. For some reason that summer I was alone on the farm with my grandparents. In the evening, after supper, I would go out and sit on the top step of the porch. I knew Grandpa would soon come out and sit on the swinging chair. He might rummage through the newspaper for a while, but soon enough he would lay it aside. After a bit Grandma would come. She would take her place beside Grandpa on the swing. And there we would sit—for hours. And oftentimes, never a word would be said. And I felt *wonderful!* It was only years later that I understood what was going on. This couple who had been together for thirty some years had no need for words. It had all been said. They were content just to be together in love. And that very complete love was embracing this little grandchild sitting on the top step. And I am sure in the midst of us was the God who is love.

Yes, we sit quietly, restfully, my Beloved and I. Thoughts arise, memories come up. I let them flow away, like so many dreams. And with them flow away the tensions, the pains, hurts that might surround them. It is the "healing of memories." It can stretch on and on. I come back refreshed.

This way of sitting with the Friend, listening to him, or just being with him, is in fact a very traditional way of prayer, one of the most ancient. Being with Jesus as a friend, talking to him as a friend, listening to him: this is prayer. It is as simple and real as that. How our quiet hours can be filled with the enjoyment of this friendship!

Because this way of just sitting with the Lord, letting him speak to us through the Scriptures, resting with him—who has said to us: "Come to me, all of you who are working hard and carrying heavy burdens, and I will refresh you"—because it is so natural, it is not at all surprising it was the way Christians prayed even in the earliest times of the church. When seekers came to spiritual fathers and mothers, they were taught this way of prayer. In time it got capsulized in a "method." Let me share this method with you in the hope that it might be helpful, trusting that you will not make it into a project, a duty or an obligation, for yourself, but that you will enjoy it. Now that we are free from so many of the cares and responsibilities of life that have been ours over the years, we enjoy a new freedom to enjoy this friendship.

There are two different expressions of our friendship with the Lord here: one is at the level of listening and talking and exploring together; the other is at the deeper level of simply resting in faith-filled love, a prayer of being rather than a prayer of doing.

Scriptural Prayer

The first we could call scriptural prayer. It was traditionally called *lectio divina,* a Latin expression difficult to properly translate. "Divine reading" or "reading the Divine," a literal translation, hardly conveys the full import of what is going on. In any case, here is the method in three points:

1. Take the Sacred Text with reverence, sensing God's presence, and call upon the Holy Spirit for help.
2. Listen to God speaking to you through the Text and respond.
3. At the end of your time together, thank God and take some word, phrase, or thought with you from the meeting.

This "taking a word with you," letting it stay in your thoughts and even repeating it at times in your mind or on your lips, is what early Christians called "meditation," *meditatio.* The ongoing conversation is, of course, prayer.

33

Centering Prayer

Then there comes the time to let all the talk and thought and everything else go, and just rest with our Friend, our God—just be with God who dwells within. This is *contemplatio*, contemplation. Known as "Prayer of the Heart" or "Prayer in the Heart," it has been more recently called Centering Prayer. Even for this, simple as it is, I can offer three points. But please do not pay any attention to these if you do not need them or if they are not useful for you. *Just be!* Be in love. Enjoy your Beloved.

As you sit, relaxed and quiet:

1. Be in faith and love with God who dwells in the center of your being.
2. Use a little love word: let it be gently present, supporting your being with God in faith-filled love.
3. Whenever you become aware of other things—thoughts, memories, or such—use your little word of love to return to resting with God.

You might like to end your time of resting with the Lord by praying very slowly and meditatively the prayer that he himself taught us, *Our Father.*

Well, I have gone on long enough here. I should leave you free now to rest a bit with the Lord. God loves us so very, very much. And God wants our happiness and fulfillment far more than we do. So relax. Enjoy the space and time that is coming into your life. Let go of the aches and pains. Dwell with the Lord on the good memories. Listen to him and let him heal the not-so-good memories. Rest with him and let him refresh—yes, make you fresh again with the joy and enthusiasm of a springlike love.

And when you are with the Lord, put in a good word for me. Thanks!

3

MY AUNT'S BELT

CLARENCE LIU

Hawai'i is my home. Its name is derived from what the ancient peoples who first came to these shores said to evoke the spiritual presence they encountered: *ha* (feminine expression of spirit), *wai* (fresh water), *i* (spiritual emotions or elemental waters). I sense this presence today in the luminous blue-green ocean that surrounds my island home. I still get "chicken skin" when I hear Hawai'i pronounced reverently by elders.

I am the chaplain in a psychiatric facility nestled in the Windward slopes of an ancient volcano. One side of the crater collapsed after the island forced its way up from the ocean floor, due to the erosion of the elements and the ceaseless pounding of the ocean; the other side of the crater, today, is the Ko'olau mountain range that extends the length of the island. Here, bamboo groves once thrived resilient and impenetrable, from which the area derived its name, Kane'ohe. It is an appropriate metaphor for the residents of the hospital, who have survived unspeakable histories and social stigma; the most seriously ill will never be able to function outside its walls.

I cherish the "holy land" of my birth. For the indigenous people of Hawai'i, the earth is alive and mother of us all. A whole ethic of caring *(malama 'aina)* for all of life is derived from this relationship. But it springs first from experiencing the temperate confluence of wind, tide, and earth that has nurtured and

35

shaped a harmonious society out of the divergent tribes that have ventured to these shores.

The power of this gentle and mystic land embraced my Asian family together with wave upon wave of immigrants from other lands who came here during the last century to begin life anew. In turn, the newcomers left their imprint upon the land and her peoples with rich festivals, customs, foods, and music. I feel proudest when I am called "local boy." A "local" is one who lives and feels this connection with the people and the land. It is what births the Aloha spirit.

Today, my heart is filled with these thoughts. A light mist blows gently down the Nu'uanu valley above Honolulu, enveloping the small gathering of my family at the grave of my aunt. At eighty-eight she had suffered an acute cerebral hemorrhage and died eight days earlier. In the windy cemetery, I am reciting the prayers for the dead with half attention. A death in the family has the effect of shipwrecking us on separate islands, removing us from the commerce of our daily lives. Here in the last half of my life, a certain disquiet has emerged belying the easy confidence of my words. Out of the corner of my eye, I see my parents, frail and slightly bent, slowly being enveloped by the soft mountain drizzle, and I wonder when we will be standing here again in this too familiar ritual.

My mind is a blur of pictures of the final night I was with her, her once ample build by then reduced to flesh and bone, holding her comatose hand in the emergency room and hoping she'd know I was there amid the trauma of hospital technology. There! I felt a slight return squeeze to my hand. Or did the finality of death open up secret worlds of grief encoded in our genes as surely as the DNA that first gave form to us? In a PBS special, "The House of Brede," a Benedictine postulant recounts her thoughts at the wake for her religious superior: grief is like a chain. At first our tears are for the deceased, then slowly we discover we are weeping for ourselves, and for all whom we've lost.

Each of us is silent, lost in our own island of grief. I look up the valley, and the sheets of mist drifting down the lush razorback mountain range strike me with their infinite beauty.

Through the mists I reenter the old family home where my aunt grew up. When I was a child it seemed cavernous, with many rooms for the once large family. It seems museum-like since they left. There is a large sitting room into which sunlight never penetrates, with straight-backed wooden rocking chairs and covered furniture. A certain stillness shrouds the rooms empty of the laughter and squeals of children once at play.

The house is a metaphor for the hidden, inner life of my aunt, which we never viewed. Even in the end when I became her primary caregiver she remained stoic, distant, and unknown. Her wish was to preserve her independence. Initially, in my zeal to take over her care, I was an intruder. I needed to quiet my own anxiety. Later, I learned to follow her lead without interfering.

After her death, in cleaning out her apartment, I discovered her clerk's skills still evidenced in the neatly organized bundles of memoirs, bank statements, and correspondence in plastic shopping bags. In paging through old family albums, I pick my way through her life chronicled in stark, yellowed black and white pictures. She is easy to identify as she peers out at me through the hard stare of a child who never knew childhood. Who was she, this solemn-faced girl, and what stories never shared did she take with her into her perfect sleep?

In front of the large house was the small, fifteen-by-twenty-foot family grocerette and snack shop. My grandpa opened it in 1914, built it for $200 then, after coming to these islands in 1889 as part of a large Chinese immigration from the Guangdong province in southern China. The "chink store" was at first eyed suspiciously by the nearby private school founded by ethnocentric New England missionaries. But it soon became a favorite hangout for the multi-ethnic neighborhood schoolchildren, predating the popular drugstore soda fountains that would come years later. Tuna sandwiches and crackseed, a popular Chinese preserve, at ten cents were a favorite, washed down with five-cent sodas. In 1975 when the store closed, four thousand kids threw a block party in appreciation.

As children, my brother, sister, and I would spend hours in the store on rainy days, sprawled out on the floor or old wooden benches reading comics while my grandpa smoked hand-rolled cigarettes in coarse brown paper and listened to Cantonese radio. At lunchtime my aunt would call us in for our favorite lunch, canned salmon on hot, streaming rice! The smell of new-fallen rain and tobacco can instantly evoke those familiar afternoons. One of the oldest of seven children, my aunt assumed responsibility for the family at an early age when my grandmother died an untimely death. There was an implicit understanding that she and her older sister would be "mother," looking after my grandfather and the boys. Although the boys had the prominent roles in the Chinese home, she never begrudged them but tended to them with an older sister's affection, and in time became our doting "maiden" aunt.

Later, when her older sister fell ill, she watched over her dying as well. She had a professional career—she was a clerical worker for the local utility company—but there was never thought of pursuing her own private ambitions. The latter were not part of her world. The social nature of her Asian identity rooted in family well-being seems quaintly outdated to my generation centered on self-actualization and personal fulfillment. In her mid-years, she had been a tall woman with a dignified bearing and dark hair pulled back into a matronly bun. Recently, as she became more bent, frozen in a permanent stoop, she refused, though physically able, to leave the apartment where she lived by herself. This decline altered her mood and appearance, but was never fully able to extinguish the glint in her eyes and her mischievous smile.

She was not used to being kissed. When I would politely peck her cheek I would come away with a smudge on my glasses from her makeup, like a silent protest of her discomfort. Her face was heavily coated with powder to hide a dark facial birthmark in a human and frail attempt to cover over the parts of ourselves we are not at home with.

Her pride showed itself in other ways. Two years ago at an annual Christmas dinner the table conversation suddenly evolved into a discussion on the precise date of my grandpa's death. Abruptly, all at the table turned to her as the oldest in the family. She didn't immediately answer. Inquiries were repeated that mounted in volume. Was she trying to remember, or did she need the long-resisted hearing aid? She remained stone-faced and unresponsive. Later that evening as I was driving her home she leaned over to me in the darkness and whispered, "You know, I don't remember when Grandpa died." She could not allow us to know that her memory was failing. Although she never married, a suitor appeared one day and in time became a "distant uncle" at family gatherings. The ongoing nature of their relationship was never publicly questioned but simply accepted in the manner of families who make silent agreements about what not to ask. I harbor a secret admiration that, for all of my aunt's restraint and observation of the conventions of the time, a part of her swam against the current, probably in the end at much personal cost to herself.

This came home to me years later when I resigned as Vicar General of the Diocese. I had been a priest for twenty years in our island church and, though I am at home in the Catholic tradition, I knew a dis-ease in the pit of my stomach that gave me no rest. Finally, when my health would no longer sustain my rationalizations for continuing, I resigned. For several years I wandered about, cut adrift without a compass, seeking to unravel the knot within.

During this period, my aunt was the epitome of acceptance. Not being a Catholic, she never understood my entering the seminary in high school as was the practice of the church in

1950. If she questioned my decision, I never knew it, but she quietly let it be known that she was willing to pay for my education if I wanted to pursue another direction. Later, when I married, she was one of the first to embrace Pat, my new wife. It was an awkward time for us all. She never hesitated. After her death, on going through old family records, I discovered that I was married on the exact date that my grandparents had married in 1905. I wonder about the symmetry she saw in all this and whether that had something to do with her acceptance. In the time that has elapsed since her death, I have often thought of the words Jesus spoke to Peter at the end of John's Gospel: "When you were younger, you used to fasten your own belt and to go wherever you wished. But when you grow old, you will stretch out your hands, and someone else will fasten a belt around you and take you where you do not wish to go" (John 21:18).

My aunt's death, like Peter's belt, has taken me to places within myself where I would rather not go. When I was young, so full of myself, I was at war with everyone, including myself. I rushed headlong into the future, confident that I knew what needed to be done. Nothing was right, and I knew how to set things straight. Now, at fifty-two, and with her death, I am not so sure. I did shape some of my future by decisions made half understood, but now the "pull" of so many other forces draws me forward with a momentum not entirely of my own making.

Did I make the right choices? Have I really loved? What regrets, like my aunt, will I take with me into that dark night? And what is that restlessness in my bones that keeps me constantly on edge? Can it be that what shadows me daily is a "wound of mortality"? Life's uncertainty principle? It was with these questions, made more urgent by my aunt's death, that I stumbled upon some words of theologian John S. Dunne that give me pause and a strange comfort:

> I had a dream in which I asked the question, "Do we love with a love we know or with a love we do not know?" And the answer

came, "with a love we do not know." I saw myself and all of us as unknowing lovers of God, led on by our heart's longing from one thing to another, from one person to another. (*Love's Mind: An Essay on Contemplative Life*, p. vii)

Somehow the notion of being an "unknowing lover of God," as I have followed the labyrinthine longings of my heart, names the journey within all of my journeys. In my struggle and restless seeking, can it be that it was I who was being sought, unknowing, until I was drawn here by my aunt? I have still not completely laid down my arms, but I am learning to trust that my crooked ways and my feeble attempts at loving may perhaps be God's unconditional loving of me.

The beach is calm tonight. The moonlight plays off small whitecaps as the waves crest and expend themselves. The warm salt waters rush up the long stretch of beach to my feet and recede back into the darkness. The soothing sound of waves along the beach is reassuring. I look up into the night sky and see a star whose dazzle has traveled light-years to greet me. It's my aunt winking. The comforting smell of steaming rice and canned salmon floats on the salty air.

4

A SPIRITUALITY OF AGING?

MONICA FURLONG

I am not too sure that there is such a thing as a "spirituality of aging." There is simply the sort of spirituality that may, or may not, have helped us during the rest of our lives, and in old age we must do the best we can with the wisdom and knowledge we have managed to cobble together in our variously misspent lives. Old age, in this as in other respects, has its advantages and disadvantages. Its advantages, spiritually speaking, may be to be spared some of the huge time pressures of younger people. In the space that was once filled with work or child-rearing, there may be more opportunity for quietness, for thinking, for meditating, for reading, at least for those who have learned a little about how to appreciate such things. More opportunity too, for those with grandchildren, to glimpse at secondhand some of the wonder with which a small child sees the world—to remember that water or a flower or an animal or the clouds are amazing in their beauty and complexity.

One of the advantages of age, I believe, is that the choices are so much fewer. The daydreams of a lifetime of finding the perfect relationship, of becoming rich or famous or phenomenally successful, of making pots of money, are taken away. It's too late. What you see is what you've got, and the Walter Mitty dreams have become irrelevant. You might as well get on and enjoy what is actually there—a practice that, in my view, is the very heart of spirituality.

But then there are the disadvantages of age—the aches and pains, the illnesses, the awareness that the number of years before death are not uncounted, as they once seemed to be, and the struggle to live on what, in many cases, is a much smaller income. There may be a failure of the sexual pleasure that once made life rich, or the loss of a partner or friends who made things feel worthwhile—what Teilhard de Chardin called "diminishments." The young, without noticing it, are slightly patronizing of the slownesses and frailties of age, and find it hard to believe in the intensity of elderly emotions. Unwittingly they cut off old people, and confine them to a loneliness of "being different," out of the swim of the mainstream of life. Power is important in our society. Most old people no longer have power, and are frequently made to feel it.

All this is painful, either in the literal sense, or in the sense of humiliation. Painful too are certain memories of times past— roads we never took, relationships we never dared, jobs in which we failed, mistakes and follies and accidents and genuine lack of opportunity, which return along with feelings of envy or rage or disappointment. If only . . . I had been born at another time, in another place, I had been thinner, fatter, taller, shorter, cleverer, more sociable, my parents had been different, I had worked harder at school, I had married a different man/woman . . . and so on. It is tempting to feel envious of the young, many of whom have opportunities that we older people did not, and who, in any case, have most of their lives to live.

Nearer, and more searching than any of this, is the fear of death. Perhaps only those in great physical pain or total despair do not fear death. For the rest of us, particularly in old age, it is a subject of speculation. How do we do it? In the words of one old lady I knew who began to be frightened, as her ninetieth birthday passed, whether she had somehow failed to die when she should have, "How do I get out?"

It's a good question. Will it be slow and painful, a cruel and exhausting struggle, or will it be sudden and unexpected, the idea bringing with it silly ideas of neighbors finding that we haven't done the washing up, picked up our clothes in the bedroom, cleaned the washbasin recently? There are other alarming possibilities of dementia, of making life a burden for one's children, of neither being able to care for oneself nor to be adequately cared for by others. Or of dying alone and slowly, with no one there to ease one's passing.

So what comfort is there in the light of all this? I remember finding a certain comfort in childbirth, as I anticipated it for the first time. Totally strange and unknown as giving birth appeared to me, I found it a help to remember that it had happened millions of times before, to women no stronger or braver than I, indeed that everyone who had ever come into the world was the result of someone undergoing what I was just about to undergo. It was normal, it was human, and it was therefore somehow bearable and possible.

I think now that there are more similarities between death and giving birth than I saw at the time. In both cases we have to surrender control to the life force within us, and trust it to know better than we do. In both cases if we fight it it hinders the process. It is our task, our purpose, our *nature* to trust and go with it, as I have sometimes watched animals do with great grace. Many cultures, particularly preindustrial ones, seem to find death easier than we do. They see death as a sort of birth, a coming into a new state. For the baby, being born is a scary process that feels like death, but it can no longer continue in the haven of the womb because it no longer fits there.

Sometimes I have thought that the right time to die may be the point at which we no longer fit into this world—when we have, in a sense, grown out of it and its preoccupations with the same handful of obsessions—money and fame and sex and love. These things may begin to strike us as so paltry, so ephemeral, that they cease to interest us enough for us to bother with them anymore. It is as if, as we begin to notice death on the far horizon, our sense of time begins to change, and we move into the gear of eternity.

If death is a sort of surrender, then there is not too much we can do about it in advance, except to think about it now and then with a friendly interest—to get beyond seeing it as an enemy and to look squarely at our fear. This is where friends who are also old are such a help. Therapists may have enough experience of the old to be very good at empathizing, and have great wisdom about the process of aging. Younger people with the right sort of sensitivity may be good at making the imaginative effort to guess what age feels like. Yet in the end they do not stand in the shoes of the elderly (and the young may be more useful keeping old people in touch with the contemporary world than trying to imagine what age feels like). For my money, it is the elderly friend who glancingly, often when we are busy with something else, tells me of his fear of another stroke or his problem about continuing to live alone, the woman friend who mentions her fear of death or of the encroaching loss of memory or hearing. Those people in fact minister most effectively to me, in a precious moment of sharing as we mutually recognize the common shame and glory of our frail humanity. Such moments of emptiness clear a path for me to unburden myself in return. Often, I notice, we end up laughing, as if there is also something irresistibly comic about our predicament. I am not quite sure what it is, but it has a healing quality.

By the same token one of the pains of aging is watching friends die one by one, each of them reducing the opportunity of sharing memories about the past, as well as fears and doubts about the present. It is a huge assault upon one's sense of identity. This is where memory helps, I think, and why old people treasure it so much. It is a kind of hump in which we store recollections of happiness, of being loved, of people and places that were dear to us, of pleasure and success in work, of the joys of child-rearing. If our present life is rich and fulfilling—and it is partly our responsibility to see that it continues to be so—then we may not need to resort to the hump of memory all that often. But in moments of sadness, fear, self-doubt, its contents may become precious to us.

Mostly, however, the question for the old is the same question that occupies everyone else—how to live while the breath is still in our lungs and the blood in our veins. There are peculiar temptations of age—laziness, passivity, timidity—which can bog us down in a tetchy kind of sloth. My heart always sinks when I hear old people coming out with their alibis for not living: "I never go out at night," "Learning is so difficult when you're older," "I never stay up that late," "I can't eat *a, b,* or *c,*" or making it clear that they long ago gave up trying to use their brains, to listen to people they disagree with, or to read anything except trashy novels. I have this revolutionary idea that old age is about living dangerously—you have less to lose than the young, after all—trying out new learning, ideas, and friends. I think of a friend in his late seventies who is still going gliding, despite two serious operations, or of my lunchtime French class, in which the average age must be about sixty-five. I love the enthusiasm of those learners, all keen to enjoy more holidays in France and to speak decent French when they do so. Three years ago I camped, with friends, on the shores of the Red Sea, and then in a series of stops across the Sinai desert. The ground was hard, the walking quite tough, and I was wiped out when I got home, but it was a lovely expedition in wilderness country. I trust it was not my last such journey. Discomfort doesn't matter, even pain (up to a point) does not matter, one's timidity does not matter. What matters is living, and living more abundantly, as Jesus said. We lived abundantly on that trip.

Yes, I know that lack of money does inhibit many things we would all like to do in age, but the spirit of adventure finds many outlets, not all of them expensive. One of the things I enjoy is startling, even shocking, the young as I do things or study things they have not thought of. It's a cheap triumph, but one I relish. With or without money, I believe that feeling *stretched*, at least sometimes, is important to human beings and their self-esteem. Whatever our age, we need to live to our fullest capacity.

Part of what makes it possible to live vigorously for as long as we can is making a real effort to maintain strength and fitness. In a way that would never have occurred to me when I was young, a simple set of physical exercises has become part of a morning meditation practice (of a very modest kind). It works out at something like twenty minutes of stretching—I follow a video tape—and ten minutes of breathing meditation. Churchgoing apart, this more or less *is* my entire spiritual practice, not count- ing (as perhaps one should) ordinary living, and at the moment I am pretty happy with it. I also make some effort to eat a bal- anced diet and to take some walking exercise. Sometimes I swim.

What I realize is also very important to me is feeling useful. Because my grandchildren are still very young, I have little doubt that I *am* useful, indeed indispensable, as a baby-sitter, counselor on sudden crises, and childminder. My own grandparents played a very important role in my young life, mainly in finding me interesting and wonderful as only grandparents can, and I feel that I can pass this precious gift to a new generation. Because I am less embroiled in the day-to-day pressures of caring for tiny children, I feel freer to watch the weekly changes and advances in growth and ability, and to marvel all over again at the aston- ishing miracle of human development. I also feel that I have at the moment a kind of leadership role in the family if I choose to exercise it. I suppose *matriarch* is the word for what I am now. It is at my home that most family celebrations take place, and, because my children are so hard-pressed with caring for *their* chil- dren, it is usually I who do the cooking, which I enormously enjoy. It is a source of real delight to me that I am, in this way, the center of the family, although I know that in time I must yield this particular responsibility to others. But at present it feels a good way of keeping the family in touch with one another, and of watching the youngest members of it enjoy being a part of it all.

Other ways of feeling useful are important to me too. I like earning money (and spending it); I like working for causes I believe in; I like feeling that people of different ages trust me enough to talk to me about things that matter to them. I resist the idea that old people need a lot of looking after. Some of them do, of course, but only for the things they really cannot manage for themselves. I like to think I am quite good at asking for help—usually for lugging heavy bags of garden compost around—when I need it.

To sum up, being old has the same spiritual problems as the rest of life, only more so—that is to say, fear, envy, and a longing for love. There is often the advantage of more free time for those who can take pleasure in it, and there is the disadvantage of increasing disability for almost everybody who survives long enough. There is love; this is the paradox of life, for those who know how to find it, which is by caring for others and allowing themselves to be vulnerable. What I believe can redeem old age, as indeed the whole of life, is a passionate commitment to living as fully as possible, whatever the restrictions; to enjoying whatever is there to be enjoyed; to laughing at whatever is there to be laughed at. Intensity is what matters.

For me, religion offers the spice that gives life a vivid flavor. I do not know that this is for everyone, but others also have their paths, their ways, their journeys, which are opaque and mysterious to me. My conviction is that life is wonderful, even when it is painful and difficult, and that the spiritual path is about knowing this (or it is useless). I have a hope that death may turn out to be wonderful too.

5

IT TAKES A LONG TIME TO BECOME YOUNG

DONALD J. SHELBY

A certain writer confessed what many have experienced:

When I was in school and college I was troubled by my young-looking face. I used to peer closely in the mirror to find the first crinkling of the skin under my eyes. I thought this would make me look older and suggest how much I had suffered. My father had several deep wrinkles in his face, and I knew, since I looked exactly like him, that these would appear on my face sooner or later and I watched for the first signs.

A few years later I peered into the same mirror trying to smooth away the dark circles and creases. I watched my hairline recede. I did daily calisthenics to keep trim, but had to admit that a 28" waist was irrecoverable. The slope down which I was clearly starting was no longer desired or welcomed.[1]

Most persons are anxious about growing older. Some would ignore it or try to conceal it. Others fight it, avoid it, or do anything but admit and accept it—especially so in our culture that prizes youthfulness. Creating a youthful appearance is big business today. It is for sale everywhere—in department stores, in beauty salons, at health spas, on TV commercials. Stylish clothes, plastic surgery, wrinkle creams, esoteric diets, magic potions to make eyes brighter, teeth whiter, hair thicker and darker, along with surefire ways to make your stature taller, your body thinner or fatter—all of these and more are purveyed. Eager customers spend billions of dollars in order to retain the appearance of younger years and stave off the effects of aging.

The apostle Paul endorsed another approach and wrote to his fellow believers in Corinth:

> Though our outer nature is wasting away, our inner nature is being renewed every day. For this slight momentary affliction is preparing for us an eternal weight of glory beyond all comparison, because we look not to the things that are seen but to the things that are unseen; for the things that are seen are transient, but the things that are unseen are eternal. (2 Corinthians 4:16-18 RSV)

By this Paul declares that whereas aging and its changes are inevitable, they need not be calamitous. They can instead be opportunities for deeper spiritual awareness, greater understanding, and livelier fulfillment. The Bible makes plain that vision and bold faith are not limited to those under thirty. In fact God often summoned those who were near or beyond their "threescore and ten" to be agents of divine truth and purpose: Abraham and Sarah, Noah, Hannah, Naomi, Zechariah and Elizabeth, Simeon and Anna, Nicodemus. The prophet Joel saw it and sang,

> I will pour out my spirit on all flesh;
> your sons and your daughters shall prophesy,
> *your old men shall dream dreams,*
> and your young men shall see visions.
> (2:28, italics added)

Dreams, visions, and conquests of the spirit are not a matter of chronological age. It isn't the number of candles on one's birthday cake, but the candlepower of one's faith. We may have experienced the passing of many summers and winters and still know a "springtime" of the spirit.

In 1966 a retrospective of the artist Picasso's works in chrono-

logical sequence was exhibited at Cannes. Hundreds of paint-
ings, from the first Picasso did as an adolescent beginner to the
latest experiments of the eighty-five-year-old master, lined the
walls. Picasso himself roamed the gallery and enjoyed the show
more than anyone. A woman stopped him one day and asked, "I
don't understand. Over there, the beginning works—so mature,
serious and solemn—then the later ones, so different, so irre-
pressible. It almost seems the dates should be reversed. How do
you explain it?"

"Easily," replied Picasso, his eyes sparkling. "It takes a long
time to become young."[2] Yes! Although our outer nature (these
bodies of ours) waste away, our inner nature (our spirits, our
souls) is constantly being renewed and refreshed. Two soundings
of this truth amplify this.

First, there is a biological aging for all of us and we must
accept it. These bodies of ours do wear out and we grow old physically as Paul said. The psalmist put it in majestic cadence:

> Thou dost sweep men away; they are like a dream,
>   like grass which is renewed in the morning:
> in the morning it flourishes and is renewed;
>   in the evening it fades and withers. . . .
> The years of our life are threescore and ten,
>   or even by reason of strength fourscore . . .
> they are soon gone, and we fly away.
>   (Psalm 90:5-6, 10 RSV)

No one has yet succeeded where Ponce de Leon failed—to
find a "fountain of youth," I mean. Even with the amazing
advances in medical science and health care, our bodies can only
last about 145 years (some experts now claim 160 years). For
most, however, genetic makeup and the wear and tear and stress
upon our bodies make for a much shorter span. But whatever the
length of that span, the unmistakable symptoms of aging finally
appear for all of us and we must accept them as gracefully as we
can. Growing older is an inevitable fact of being alive, and the

greater our acceptance of it, the more joy and meaning we find in the process.

There was once a couple who lived in a California retirement complex. For thirty years the man was editor of a major magazine. The Christmas letters that this couple wrote to their friends were such gems that they found their way into print and wide distribution. One read as follows:

At 86, Rosie and I live by the rule of the elderly. If the toothbrush is wet, you have brushed your teeth. If the bedside radio is warm in the morning, you know you left it turned on all night. If you realize you are wearing one black and one brown shoe, you know you have a pair like it somewhere in the closet. I stagger when I walk and small boys follow me making bets on which way I'll veer next. I remember the friend who told me years ago, "If your I.Q. ever breaks 100, sell." On my daily excursions I greet everyone, including the headrests in parked empty cars. Dignified friends seem surprised when I salute them with a breezy "Hi!" They don't realize that I haven't got breath for a two-syllable greeting.[3]

What a delightful attitude! To accept the process of aging and be able to find humor in it while affirming the wonder and beauty of it keeps life a joy rather than a burden. When Philip Halsman came to photograph the Italian movie actress Anna Magnani, he went to some lengths to warn her, "My lens is very sharp and it will show all the lines in your face, but I'll try to minimize them as best I can and will touch up what appear." "Don't hide them," the actress said. "I went through too much to get them." We can celebrate the struggles and victories that are etched in our faces and on our souls rather than apologize or be embarrassed by them. We can be grateful that the years of our life have been so active and full that parts of us are wearing out. Only then shall we be ready to savor the unique rewards that come with increased age.

While there is a biological aging and "our nature wastes away," there is also spiritual aging, which makes us grow younger with the passing years. That is the second sounding. Our inner nature can continually be renewed if we take time to let that happen to us. When those who are under thirty are blowing "Taps" in cynical dismissal of the world's chaos and contradictions, those who have lived long enough to grow young in spirit blow "Reveille" because they know that the present darkness is transitory. They know that God is never without divine witness or saving remnant and that the deepest contradictions are never beyond God's persuasion and saving power of love. That is why those who are young in spirit can face the future and believe the best is yet to be.

To be hopeful, creative, refreshed, open, concerned, aware, expectant is to be young in spirit. We may be old in body but young in soul if we let God nurture in us through the years the thirst for learning and the spirit of kindness, love, beauty, goodness, and justice. If we have walked with God when we could, we shall still keep going on even when our legs are weak, our joints ache, our eyesight dims, and we do not hear as well as we used to.

Think how long it took John Milton's spirit to come to that place where he could write *Paradise Lost,* J. S. Bach's spirit to utter the *Goldberg* Variations, Beethoven's spirit to soar in his Ninth Symphony, or Wagner's spirit to create *Parsifal.* Think of the years it took for Michaelangelo's spirit to become young enough to create *The Last Judgment* and design St. Peter's in Rome.

It takes a long time to become young! Picasso was right. Aging is part of that spiritual journey we all make—a very important part. Our faith in God that believes that God's love is at work in us and around us can keep us young in spirit through all the seasons of life. A few days after his inauguration as President of the United States in 1933, Franklin Roosevelt paid a call on Justice Oliver Wendell Holmes, Jr., aged ninety-two. He found the justice sitting in his library reading Plato. Following a few pleasantries, the President said, "May I ask why you're reading Plato,

Mr. Justice?" To which he replied, "Certainly, Mr. President. To improve my mind!"

And we could add, to stay young in spirit, to stay alert, and growing on into a future where the best is yet to be!

Notes

1. Thomas Howard, *Christ the Tiger* (San Francisco: Ignatius Press, 1990).
2. Garson Kanin, *It Takes a Long Time to Become Young* (Garden City, N.Y.: Doubleday, 1978).
3. Clarence Forsberg (United Methodist minister, retired), *Newsletter*.

6

DO YOU KNOW WHAT TIME IT IS?

A Meditation on Romans 13:8-14

JAMES A. HARNISH

You could call it Millennium Fever. Everyone, it seems, is watching the time, counting down the days until the calendar page flips over to the year 2000. At Great Britain's Royal Greenwich Observatory, a numbered counter straddling the prime meridian clicks off the countdown in hundredths of a second. In Paris, the days tick by on a 50-ton, 1,342-light sign that hangs from the second level of the Eiffel Tower.

More entrepreneurial timekeepers are constantly discovering ways to make money from the countdown. Branco International offers a waterproof "Third Millennium Challenge" wristwatch, which counts off the remaining seconds of the twentieth century. For the global traveler, a desktop timepiece from Countdown Clocks International announces the time remaining before "The Dawn of a New Millennium"; this clock can be adjusted for any of the world's time zones. All of us—for a price!—can know exactly what time it is today in relation to that day in the future when we cross over into the third millennium.

In a similar way, the first Christians measured time in relation to the *parousia,* the final day when they would cross over into the fulfillment of God's saving purpose for human history. They counted the days of their lives in relation to their expectation of an immediate return of Christ.

But as the years passed and the pile of discarded calendar

57

pages began to grow, they were forced to rethink the timing of the promised return of Christ. The first generation of Christians began to die of old age, still waiting for the day of the Lord to come. The reality of an aging church required them to shift from the expectation of an immediate return of Christ to a life of faith that looked forward to the final day but lived every day with a sense of divine urgency. They shaped their lives around the expectation that the day of the Lord was always at hand.

That spirit of divine urgency underlies Paul's stirring wake-up call to the Roman Christians. "You know what time it is, how it is now the moment for you to wake from sleep. For salvation is nearer to us now than when we became believers; the night is far gone, the day is near" (Romans 13:11-12). While still counting the days until God's saving purpose would be completed in the future, Paul declared that the time to put away the works of darkness and live in the light is now! God's gift of salvation is not reserved for a final day somewhere in the future. It can become a formative reality in the present life of every follower of Christ.

Contemporary reflection on the spiritual shift that occurred in the aging process in the early church may be a stirring wake-up call for people in every generation. The aging process and a keen awareness of our mortality can awaken within us a vibrant sense of God's saving presence in every day of our lives.

I was visiting a church member in the cardiac unit of the local hospital. His bypass surgery had been a success; he would go home soon. I had sensed along the way that he found a measure of comfort in knowing that at one time I had been a cardiac patient too. When the nurse came to check his blood pressure, he introduced me by saying, "This is my pastor. He was a patient in here a year ago." More from professional courtesy, I suspect, than genuine interest, she asked, "What brought you in?"

"Cardiomyopathy," I replied. The look on her face indicated that she seriously doubted that I knew what I was talking about. More curious now, she asked her question about as directly as she could. "Really? Then why are you still here?" She explained to my surprised parishioner that most patients diagnosed with cardiomyopathy die unless they receive a heart transplant.

The diagnosis had come as a surprise. I was forty-five years old and by all signs in good health. My wife and I were rapidly approaching our twenty-fifth wedding anniversary; our daughters were in college. After twenty years of ministry, I had just made the biggest move in my career. Suddenly the book I was writing on male midlife crisis took on a whole new urgency.

The congestive heart failure that landed me in the hospital was an unwelcome interruption to a November football weekend. I had intended to be in the stadium to cheer for the University of Florida Gators on Saturday and the Tampa Bay Buccaneers on Sunday afternoon. With that in mind, a football analogy seemed the most appropriate way to describe my feelings to my twin brother. "I feel like it's halftime in the locker room," I said. "I sure hope I get to play the rest of the game, but if I don't, I've had one heck of a good first half!" The analogy expressed my gratitude for the past, my desire to live into the future, and my head-on confrontation with my mortality.

Memories of that experience flooded my brain as the nurse asked, "How is your heart doing now?" When I told her that the latest stress test revealed absolutely normal heart function, she gave me another disbelieving stare and asked, "Do you mind if I listen to your heart?" My parishioner-patient snickered like someone who already knows the punch line of a good joke as he watched me unbutton my shirt. The nurse listened to my heart and blurted out, "That's miraculous!"

It is miraculous, and I am very grateful. Five years of healthy reports have passed since that life-threatening weekend, but each checkup is a reminder that life is short. It can be taken away suddenly, when we least expect it, "in the twinkling of an eye" (1 Corinthians 15:52), in a moment of time.

I passed my fiftieth birthday this year. My skinny body is in about as good shape as it ever was. My marriage is in better shape than my body. My daughters are happily on their own. I have a deep sense of calling to the church I serve and a genuine passion about the vision to which God has called us. I am richly blessed by honest, laughter-soaked friendships. Life is very good!

But actuarial tables don't lie. I'm into the third quarter now. The countdown is on. Time is passing quickly. There are more years of ministry behind than before me. There will be fewer sermons to preach in the future than I have preached in the past. Some things I hoped to do will never be done. The reality of the aging process is sinking in. All things considered, there could hardly be a better time to reflect on the urgency with which Paul calls us to "put on the Lord Jesus Christ."

The active verb describes a conscious choice, like choosing to put on the clothing we wear. Aware of the shortness of life, the apostle challenges us to claim the presence of the risen Christ in our present experience.

L. Gregory Jones, the Dean of the Duke Divinity School, introduced me to a fascinating conversation between Alice and the Queen in *Alice in Wonderland*. Alice begins:

> "I don't care for jam."
> "It's very good jam," said the Queen.
> "Well, I don't want any *to-day*, at any rate."
> "You couldn't have it if you *did* want it," the Queen said.
> "The rule is, jam to-morrow and jam yesterday—but
> never jam *to-day*."
> "It *must* come sometimes to jam to-day," Alice objected.
> "No, it can't," said the Queen. "It's jam every *other* day:
> to-day isn't any other day, you know."

Jones wrote that "for too many of us, there is a resurrection yesterday (Jesus') and a resurrection tomorrow (the resurrection of the dead), but never resurrection today" (*The Christian Century*, July 1-8, 1992, p. 644).

The great good news that Paul proclaimed is that now is the

time for the risen Christ to be alive in our experience. Because of the resurrection, today is never just another day; this is the day of salvation. The living Christ is not imprisoned in the past or waiting for the future, but is alive with us in every phase of our lives.

Two decades have passed since my first visit to the Washington cathedral, which towers over our nation's capital on Mount St. Alban. The west facade, completed in 1990, glows in the setting sun with the purity of new-cut Indiana limestone. By contrast, the original walls of the apse and the flying buttresses of the nave show the signs of the aging process. Nearly eight decades of wind, snow, and rain are turning the cream-colored stone to brown and gray. The carved images of Jesus and the disciples over the entrance in the south transept will never recapture the purity of their original color. They are taking on a weathered maturity with the passing of the years. Even the massive figure of "Christ in Majesty" above the high altar, carved from the purist white stone in the cathedral, will take on a different appearance as it bears the effects of time.

As I observed the aging process in the walls of the cathedral, I realized the way my own relationship with Christ has changed across the years. The Christ to whom I committed my life as a child still reigns over the central altar of my life, but the rugged realities of time, the harsh hurts of broken hearts, and the windy gusts of change have brought me to a more weathered, more mature image of him. There is a deepening awareness of the absolute stability of God's unchanging presence in the changing realities of my life experience as my childhood images of Jesus age with me. My experience is that Christ ages very well!

Rembert Weakland, the Roman Catholic Archbishop of Milwaukee, acknowledged that "getting old isn't for sissies." He told the story of a woman who complained to her parish priest about her old-age aches and pains. When her pastor suggested that she remember Jesus and his suffering, the woman shot back, "Yeah, but he didn't live long enough to feel the pain of rheumatism!" (*Context,* June 1, 1997, p. 4).

She was literally correct, of course. But the resurrection means that the living Christ is present with us throughout the journey of our lives, far beyond the thirty-something years Jesus traveled the dusty roads of Palestine. There is a sense in which the living Christ ages with us. Because of the resurrection, today is never just another day. This is the day of salvation. Now is the time to put on a new, maturing relationship with Christ.

This is also the time for a new relationship with other people. The aging process and the awareness of our mortality can give new urgency to Paul's command, "Owe no one anything, except to love one another; for the one who loves another has fulfilled the law" (Romans 13:8).

I am amazed that my daughter and some of her friends still remember the words of William Sloane Coffin that I quoted at their high school baccalaureate service: "The world is too large for anything but truth and too small for anything but love."

As my hair grows both thinner and grayer and the time of my life becomes shorter, one thing becomes increasingly clear: life is too short for anything but love. Life is too short to be wasted in bitterness, hostility, and resentment. Because we know the brevity of our lives, now is the time to invest in relationships that become a human expression of the self-giving, life-transforming, hope-building love of God revealed in Jesus Christ.

I attended the funeral for the wife of a fellow pastor recently. They met in Argentina when he was a young man serving as a missionary. They were both ordained ministers and had served together until their retirement, often in very difficult places. Their life together had been a faithful journey of compassionate, Christ-like, people-loving ministry. They had shared many miles together, but they had hoped for many more.

As I watched him stand to sing the opening hymn, I thought about my own marriage. I was confronted with the inescapable fact that one day, one of us will stand where he stood, the time having run out on our journey together. In that moment, I felt some small fraction of both his gratitude and pain. I also felt the deep urgency to fill the time my wife and I have together with deep love, rich laughter, and great joy. Our time together is too short for anything less. Now is the time to love one another boldly and freely in the spirit of Christ.

Now is also the time, Paul says, to "live honorably as in the day." I take that as a call to live each day as fully and richly as we can in the light of the call of God on our lives.

When Art Buchwald, the Washington humorist, delivered the commencement address at the University of Southern California, he challenged the graduates to make the most of the time in which they are living.

> I don't know if this is the best of times or the worst of times. But I can assure you of this—it's the only time you've got. So you can either stay in bed or go out and pick a daisy. . . . We seem to be going through a period of nostalgia, and everyone seems to think that yesterday was better than today. I personally don't think it was—and if you're hung up on nostalgia my advice is to pretend today is yesterday and go out and have one helluva time. (*Context*, August 15, 1993)

My midlife confrontation with my own mortality and the inescapable effect of the turning of the pages of my life's calendar have reminded me that this is the only time we have. If we know what time it is, if we realize how short life can be, if we actually believe that salvation is near, then we know that this is the only time we have to squeeze as much life as possible into every day.

I'd like to age with the same grace, joy, and faith as Waller and Doris McCleskey. Waller is past eighty now. They have been married for fifty-eight years. They never would have chosen for the final years of their life together to revolve around the schedule for his kidney dialysis, doctor appointments, and medication for heart trouble. But they are facing it with great dignity, with deep love for each other, and with an absolute passion to squeeze joy out of every day that they have. I have heard Doris say it often enough to know that it is a central affirmation of their faith: "We're just thankful for every day that we have, and we are going to make the very best of it."

They are the first to say that the strength, dignity, and joy with which they are facing the difficulties and limitations of old age are a direct result of a long life of faith. Their maturing relationship with the risen living Christ is rooted in years of faithful worship, disciplined Bible study, active fellowship with Christian friends, and soul-stretching prayer. Their faith has aged with them and continues to fill them with great love, joy, and peace.

So Paul offers his stirring call to action: "Now is the moment for you to wake from sleep. . . . Let us lay aside the works of darkness and put on the armor of light."

Alfred Lord Tennyson sounded the same call to action in his classic poem "Ulysses." The aging hero remembers his past experiences as "an arch wherethro'/Gleams that untravelled world, whose margin fades."

Then he challenges his time-tested companions.

> Come, my friends,
> 'Tis not too late to seek a newer world.
> Push off, and sitting well in order smite
> The sounding furrows; for my purpose holds
> To sail beyond the sunset and the baths
> Of all the western stars, until I die. . . .
> Though much is taken, much abides; and though
> We are not now that strength which in old days
> Moved earth and heaven, that which we are, we are;
> One equal temper of heroic hearts,
> Made weak by time and fate but strong in will
> To strive, to seek, to find, and not to yield.
> (*Theme and Form,* p. 586)

I sensed the same passion in a retired business executive who looked across my desk and said, "Jim, I've always had to do what my job demanded. Some of it was good; some of it seems very unimportant. Now that I'm retired, I get to choose where I put my energy and I want to do something that will really make a difference. I don't have time for anything else."

Knowing what time it is in our lives can become the opportunity for the Spirit of God to call us to a new way of living in relationship with the risen Christ, a new way of being in relationship with other people, and a new way of serving as people of faith.

William H. Willimon, Dean of the Chapel at Duke University, once described a funeral that he and his wife attended in a small, hot, crowded church in rural Georgia. The preacher shouted, fumed, and flailed his arms around over the casket. "It's too late for Joe," he screamed. "He's dead. It's all over for him. He might have wanted to straighten his life out, but he can't now. It's over."

Then the preacher pointed his finger at the congregation and shouted: "But it ain't too late for you! People drop dead every day. So why wait? Now is the day for decision. Now is the time to make your life count for something. Now is the time to give your life to Jesus!"

Willimon thought it was the worst funeral sermon he had ever heard and poured out his criticism to his wife on the way home. She listened patiently. She agreed that it was tacky, manipulative, and callous. But then she said, "Of course, the worst part is that it's all true" (*The Christian Century*, December 3, 1986, p. 1085).

It's all true, you know. There was no doubt in Paul's mind. The countdown is on; the calendar pages are turning at an alarming rate. The night is far gone; the day is near. We know what time it is. Now is the moment to wake up and live!

7

TURNING TOWARD HOME

PHYLLIS C. ROE

The forties are the old age of youth
While the fifties are the youth of old age.
—Victor Hugo

So tell me, what will you do with your one wild and precious life?
—Mary Oliver, poet

Our hearts are restless until they find their rest in thee.
—Augustine

Every seven seconds another person turns fifty. Next month I will be among them. As part of the Baby Boomer generation I have plenty of company in facing fifty, as an unprecedented number of us cross the half-century threshold. Even the President of the United States and the First Lady have turned fifty while in office, calling attention to the rise to leadership of our postwar generation.

At the numerous "50s" birthday parties I am invited to attend these days, I notice in our laughter and joking about aging a mixture of celebration and anxiety. There is a certain defiance in the face of our recognition that at fifty we cannot deny the passing of time and its markers of crow's feet, gray hair, and other physical changes. "If you're going to turn fifty, do something big to celebrate," many friends advise. One woman, now in her seventies and well into a flourishing second career, told me she ran her first marathon at fifty. Another friend recalls that she pasted fifty gold stars in her journal on her fiftieth birthday. Since then she has finished a Ph.D., married a second time, and is traveling around the world, reveling in meeting new people and experiencing new cultures. I read of another woman who, with only a few skiing lessons, went out on her fiftieth birthday and skied down the tallest mountain near her just to prove she could. We figuratively shake our fists in the face of our inevitable aging and celebrate being alive and having new possibilities.

Underneath the cheerful consolation our adventures and celebrations bring, however, is an anxiety. As I talk with friends and look at my own reactions, I see that we sense that Victor Hugo is right. We are entering the "youth of old age." We may not be elderly yet; but we can see from afar, and it's not as far off as it used to be. When we stop to think about it, there are moments of dis-ease, awareness of a vague restlessness, as it dawns on us that by fifty there are fewer years ahead of us than behind us. We have entered the last half, or perhaps the last third, of our lives.

Of course, this awareness is not always literally connected with turning fifty. For some it may come sooner, for others later, as Frederick Buechner describes:

> When I was young . . . I lived as though my time was endless. When I was in my fifties and early sixties even, I deluded myself with the fantasy that I was still somehow middle-aged and had roughly as much time left to live as I had lived already, which seemed endless enough for all practical purposes. But now that I find myself pushing seventy hard, I have finally begun to wise up. It is no longer just in my mind that I know I am rather a good deal closer to the end of my time than I am to its beginning. I know it in my stomach, and there is a lot of sadness in knowing it. But that is by no means all there is. Who would want it to be day forever and never night, after all? Who would choose to be awake forever and never get a chance to sleep?[1]

It is this awareness of mortality, that life has definite limits, which lends a certain urgency to decisions we make in midlife.

"To know one will die in a fortnight marvelously clarifies the mind," wrote Dr. Boswell in the eighteenth century. While hoping my death will be farther away than a fortnight, I find the recognition that life is limited to be like looking through a telescope and turning the focus knob, so that what was far away and blurry is brought close and suddenly seems very clear. We don't have forever. This is the gnawing awareness that underlies the midlife transition, at whatever age we become conscious of it.

Of course, the outer limits of life don't usually announce themselves quite as boldly as facing our death. What first gets our attention in midlife is often the experience of physical limits: menopause, which both limits the ability to bear children and frees women from the threat of pregnancy; less physical stamina and flexibility; lower metabolism; skin wrinkles; the first pair of bifocal glasses; hints of balding. Sometimes it is in our jobs or careers that we encounter limits: forced early retirement due to downsizing, being passed over when a job we wanted goes to a younger person. While some are nearing or at the peak of their careers at fifty, others are realizing they have probably gone as far as they will go in their field. In our personal lives, we run into the realization that our spouse is never going to be all we might want. Perhaps most difficult of all, we begin to recognize that no matter how hard we work, we cannot always make life come out the way we want it to. In spite of our best efforts, tragic and terrible things happen to people we love and to ourselves.

As a counselor I see the fallout from those who seek to escape the anxiety of midlife by making a desperate attempt to fight against accepting limits in life. Our society encourages us to believe we can be everything we want to be and have everything we want in life. So we go to plastic surgeons, divorce a midlife spouse to marry someone younger who can still bear children, refuse to tell anyone our age. The tragedy in this approach is that it is doomed to fail. Sooner or later, we all face the fact that life has limits.

We don't have forever. Is this all there is? What do I really want to do with the rest of my life? These are the frequent refrains of midlife, repeated with a hint or more of anxiety, unrest, and longing. It is in this very anxiety that I think the grace of midlife lies hidden, waiting to be mined for the richness it offers. If we face the truths disguised in the uneasiness of midlife, we will go a long way toward preparing ourselves to age with grace and meaning.

"Our hearts are restless until . . ." God places within our hearts a longing for connection with the larger whole, with the One who is the ground of our being and the source of meaning. The anxiety many experience at whatever age "midlife" awareness hits can act as a homing device—to guide us to that source, to turn us toward a truer sense of self and an enlarged sense of our place in the world. It can guide us home—home to our deeper self and home to God, the One in whom we live and move and have our being.

In the first half of life, we are busy creating a life for ourselves. We go to school, learn a trade, find a partner, make a home, have children, start a business, or enter a career or profession. Our focus is on the outer world and finding a place for ourselves in that world. Psychiatrist C. G. Jung was among the first to show us that in midlife there is a developmental need for energy to shift from a primary focus on the outer world to a concern with the inner world. Prompted by the awareness of time passing, we look at who we've become. In the first half of our life we chose certain paths. Now we reexamine the roads chosen and those not taken. We ask, What does it all mean?

The danger of midlife lies in stagnation—in failing to come to terms with the limitations of life and with the challenges of deepening one's inner life, becoming encapsulated by stale routines, imprisoned in unchallenging and unrewarding jobs or empty marriages or getting lost in seeking freedom from limits through addictions, affairs, or simply bolting from all responsibilities, thus increasing the risk of despair when aging becomes an inescapable fact.

The possibilities for personal transformation are ripe in midlife. We have an opportunity to reclaim values, interests, goals we had that may have been laid aside but now offer us a chance to revitalize our lives. Anxiety can become energy that shifts toward the development of inner resources, toward what is fulfilling rather than what is expected, toward what the soul needs rather than what the ego wants. With more freedom from the need to prove ourselves, to establish ourselves, which is common in the first half of life, one has the opportunity to become more fully oneself, to be more creative. There can be an inner freedom that develops as we give up trying to please everyone and find more self-definition. Along with the awareness of life's limits also comes, for many, an increasing willingness to take risks, to express our own opinions, to live for what we believe in. It can be a turning point toward greater personal wholeness as we face our inner selves, come to terms with the less recognized aspects of ourselves, and incorporate all of this into a more whole and realistic picture of who we are.

Evelyn Whitehead, a noted writer and teacher with special expertise in the field of aging, was once asked, "What is the best way to prepare for aging?" Her answer was to begin in midlife to develop a spiritual foundation. This is the time, she said, to gather resources that will sustain us through the later years of life when we may not be able to work or may be in poor health—resources of prayer and the ability to enjoy solitude, of an ability to find meaning simply in being alive and being part of creation rather than in accomplishments.[2] Midlife becomes a training ground for old age, beginning with the awareness of limits, which we begin to glimpse in the fifties. In the clarifying light of that awareness, we can see more clearly what's important. We are freed from trying to establish ourselves and drawn toward fundamental connections in which we sense a greater wholeness. If I can begin to fashion my life in response to this grace-filled awareness, then the trajectory toward old age and death seems less fearful. Spiritually I experience the search for wholeness as a search for God, a search for our true home.

For Christians it is in Jesus and in the lives that have been touched by Jesus that we are shown a way of living in this world as whole human beings. "When we glimpse that wholeness in others, we recognize it immediately for what it is, and the reason we recognize it, I believe, is that no matter how much the world shatters us to pieces, we carry inside us a vision of wholeness that we sense is our true home and that beckons us."[3] In these words, Buechner invites us to hold on to the vision of wholeness, which is the Reign of God, and to look for glimpses of that wholeness in every day of our remaining years.

Midlife offers us the opportunity and the challenge to begin turning toward that vision of wholeness and to live from that vision so that when we reach the end of our days and it is time to cross over to the next life, we will recognize that we are home.

Notes

1. Frederick Buechner, *The Longing for Home: Recollections and Reflections* (San Francisco: Harper, 1996), pp. 1-2.
2. Speech by Evelyn Whitehead at the Pacific Region, American Association of Pastoral Counselors, Conference on Aging and Spirituality, October 1996.
3. Buechner, *Longing for Home*, p. 110.

8

SARAH LAUGHED

JANE E. VENNARD

*They said to him, "Where is your wife Sarah?" And he said, "There,
in the tent." Then one said, "I will surely return to you in due season,
and your wife Sarah shall have a son." And Sarah was listening at
the tent entrance behind him. Now Abraham and Sarah were old,
advanced in age; it had ceased to be with Sarah after the manner of
women. So Sarah laughed to herself, saying, "After I have grown old,
and my husband is old, shall I have pleasure?" The LORD said to
Abraham, "Why did Sarah laugh, and say, 'Shall I indeed bear a
child, now that I am old?' Is anything too wonderful for the LORD? At
the set time I will return to you, in due season, and Sarah shall have
a son." But Sarah denied, saying, "I did not laugh"; for she was
afraid. He said, "Oh yes, you did laugh."* (Genesis 18:9-15)

*The LORD dealt with Sarah as he had said, and the LORD did for
Sarah as he had promised. Sarah conceived and bore Abraham a
son in his old age, at the time of which God had spoken to him.
Abraham gave the name Isaac to his son whom Sarah bore
him. . . . Now Sarah said, "God has brought laughter for me; everyone who hears will laugh with me." And she said, "Who would ever
have said to Abraham that Sarah would nurse children? Yet I have
borne him a son in his old age."* (Genesis 21:1-3, 6-7)

We laugh in delight. We laugh in wonder and amaze-
ment. We laugh for joy. We may laugh when we are
afraid or embarrassed or nervous. If we realize we
have laughed inappropriately we often deny that we laughed at

all. Ninety-year-old Sarah laughed in all these ways when God came to offer her the promise of fulfillment. We have much to learn about our relationship to God in our elder years from Sarah's doubt and fear, her faith and her fulfillment. Sarah's laughter holds lessons for us all.

What does it mean to be given a promise of new life when we believe our useful, creative, productive lives are over? What does it mean to discover promise in the midst of our narrow, barren lives? Although God appeared to Sarah with a clearly spoken promise, most of us are not so blessed. The absence of a clear voice can lead us to despair and fear that God's promise may be reserved for others. Our faith in God's constant all-abiding love may begin to waver. Our most frequent prayer may become: "How long, O LORD? Will you forget me forever?" (Psalm 13:1*a*).

When our lives are filled with despair, the story of Sarah and her laughter and delight can feel like a cruel joke. We read of Sarah wishing for a son and God responding with a miraculous birth. We wonder why God is not answering our prayers. We wonder why our wishes have not been granted. Although Sarah received the son she longed for, her story is not about wish fulfillment. Her story is about God's promise to be with us always. Her story is about God's constant love for all people, and the power of this love to break into our daily lives. The outpouring and inbreaking of God's love may not change our situation as it did Sarah's, but God's love can transform our hearts.

If we are willing to believe in God's promise even in the worst of times, we can open ourselves to the possibility of receiving God's gifts. God's love will slowly break open our hearts, and our way of seeing and being in the world can become new. Old problems will gradually reveal new solutions. Old worries can be seen with new eyes. Unresolved conflicts begin to untangle themselves in the presence of love. When our hearts are transformed our mouths may become filled with laughter, and our tongues with shouts of joy (Psalm 126:2*a*).

As we reflect on Sarah's story and the tale of a modern-day Sarah, do not take the events literally, but listen for the constancy of God's love that is revealed in different ways. Hear the promise that God holds for everyone. Discover the laughter and delight that is waiting for all of us when we are open to God's surprising grace.

When God came to speak to Sarah and Abraham, their lives had become narrow and set. They knew what life had given them and they hoped for nothing new. They had lived a life of barrenness so long they could imagine nothing else. They had resigned themselves to the way things were. When Sarah heard the promise that life would be different, she laughed in disbelief. This also is the life of a modern-day Sarah. Seventy years old, Sarah is confined to a wheelchair in a small airy room in a pleasant nursing home. Her husband left her, and her grown children are far away. Sarah makes the best of her narrow existence. She finds new ways to overcome her physical pain. She reads and listens to music. She visits with friends. Sarah is resigned and holds no hope for a different future.

What causes us to lose hope in a new and better future as we grow older? What happens to our faith that nothing is too wonderful for God? We often forget that God's love and promise are for all of us, no matter our age, physical ability, or station in life. We tend to believe that God fulfills other people's dreams, younger people's dreams. But the story in Genesis tells us that God is active in surprising places and surprising ways. God comes to a tired, cynical, barren old woman and turns her life upside down.

But Sarah does not believe easily. She looks at herself and at Abraham. She looks at their life in all its harshness. Sarah laughs. She laughs in disbelief and hopelessness. She mocks the message. She closes her heart to the possibility of new life. Closed too is the heart of our modern-day Sarah. She is not visited by messengers of God, but she is called on regularly by the widower of an old friend. They spend quiet hours in discussion about books and lively hours arguing about politics. Sometimes he brings flowers or her favorite candy. "He's smitten!" Sarah's friends tell her. "Oh, no," she scoffs. "He's just a lonely old man. What would he want with me and my withered legs?" Poking fun at her visitor and herself, Sarah laughs in disbelief, closing her heart in hopelessness.

Why did Sarah laugh? Why did she deny she laughed? And why did God hold her to the truth of her laughter? Scripture indicates that Sarah laughed because she did not believe that new life could come from her barren womb. She laughed in mockery of herself, her situation, and her God. When God confronted her, she was afraid, and she tried to cover her fear by lying. But God confronted her again. I imagine Sarah was left feeling sad, shaken, confused, and wondering what would happen next.

When God confronts our fear, our hopelessness, and our disbelief, we are given the opportunity to look anew at our own lives. When we hear the truth spoken in love we can examine our tightly held ideas of reality, open our blind spots to the light, and release our narrow expectations. God spoke the truth in love to Sarah. "Oh yes, you did laugh," God says. Because the truth was told, Sarah had to face her own disbelief. And in facing herself, she readied herself to receive God's gift. Speaking the truth in love comes from friends as well as from God. Our modern-day Sarah was confronted by her clergyman. Sarah was laughing about her "gentleman caller" and her friends' interpretation of his attention. "Why are you laughing, Sarah?" the minister asked her gently. "Do you believe yourself unworthy of love? Do you doubt your ability to love? Are you afraid?" Sarah has to attend to these issues if she is to be ready to receive God's gift.

"The LORD did for Sarah as he had promised" (Genesis 21:1b). Into the life of Sarah and Abraham came Isaac, meaning "the one who laughs" or "laughing boy." Sarah became the mother of laughter! Sarah's disbelief, doubt, and fear were swept away by the fulfillment of God's promise. She laughed in delight and invited the whole community to laugh with her. She was filled with wonder and gratitude at the miracle that had occurred in her life. But the miraculous conception and birth of Isaac are not the end of the story. Everything was not made easy and perfect by God's intervention in their lives. Sarah, in addition to the other tasks that were expected of her as Abraham's wife, now had a child to raise. Because of her own son and her fear for his inheritance, Sarah became jealous of Abraham's firstborn and ordered him to send the child and his mother, Hagar, away. Abraham was distressed at this turn of events and resisted Sarah's order, following through only at God's insistence (Genesis 21:8-12).

And can you imagine how Sarah felt when Abraham set forth with her son, Isaac, to offer him as a burnt offering? (Genesis 22:1-2). God may have spoken directly to Abraham who was ready to obey, but what was this like for Sarah? Isaac's birth brought new struggle and pain into Abraham's and Sarah's lives. I imagine all was not easy in their household.

Sarah of this century also turned her laughter of disbelief into laughter of joy and delight. Her friends and her minister were right. This good man wished to marry her. They had a small ceremony with much celebration and laughter. They felt God's presence in and among them. "A miracle!" Sarah was heard to exclaim. "Who would have believed that I would find love so late in my life?" But all was not easy with the new couple. Money was scarce and both of them had health problems. Although they got a larger apartment at the nursing home, there was not a lot of space. Their grown children were not happy with the new marriage and for quite a while were not helpful to their parents. This miracle of love caused Sarah struggle and pain as well as delight.

These Sarah stories are not about "happily ever after." They are not about God making everything perfect. These stories are a reminder that God is with us, God loves us, and that "we are not bounded by necessity but by the freedom of God's love, offered in faithfulness" (Brueggemann, p. 182). God moves both Sarahs beyond their narrow expectations, their resignation to life as it is, and their disbelief. Through promise and confrontation, God moves them beyond themselves into a new place and a new experience of laughter. God's promise is for all of us. We are not bounded by necessity. We are held by the freedom of God's love. We might scoff; we might doubt; we might laugh in disbelief. But God has a way of breaking through our hardened hearts to bring miracles into our lives.

These miracles may not be as surprising as the birth of a child in our ninetieth year or even the appearance of a new mate. The miracle may be as small and as simple as a new idea read in an old book that helps us see life anew. The surprise might be the sudden courage to take a class on journal writing and the strength to put pen to paper after all these years. The surprise might be the gift of a tape recorder and easy access to books on tape when we think our reading days are over.

When we recognize and accept the miracles that enter our lives, we are called to laughter—laughter of delight, laughter of wonder, laughter of sheer joy. Then, like Sarah, we can speak the words of gratitude: "God has brought laughter for me, [and] everyone who hears will laugh with me."

Resources

Walter Brueggemann, *Genesis. Interpretation: A Bible Commentary for Teaching and Preaching,* James Luther Mays, ed. (John Knox Press, 1982).

Ellen Frankel, *The Five Books of Miriam: A Woman's Commentary on the Torah* (G. P. Putnam's Sons, 1996).

9

FOR EVERYTHING THERE IS A SEASON

GENE M. TUCKER

Our experience of and attitude toward aging are distinctly related to our experience of and attitude toward the natural world. All things in nature are subject to the vicissitudes of time; most living things grow old, and all eventually die. Moreover, our experience of and attitude toward aging are shaped by our religious life and experience. For Christians and Jews, and to a certain extent all who have been touched by Western culture, that religious life is shaped to a greater or lesser degree by the biblical tradition. Consequently, one way to reflect upon aging is to consider the natural world and the Old Testament views of both aging itself and the relationship of human beings to the rest of creation.

One of my earliest memories is of the night sky over the desert of West Texas. I looked at stars beyond number, reaching from horizon to horizon, with a sense of awe and wonder. That sky also evoked my first theological questions: How vast and wonderful this world is, more than I can understand, and what is beyond the stars in that sky? What is the meaning of human life in such an awesome environment?

I do not remember a time when I did not view the natural world with a sense of wonder. Not always delight, to be sure, for I have seen the tornado, feared the snowstorm, shuddered at reports of earthquakes, and even complained about the weather.

As I grow older that sense of wonder only seems to increase. I know more, recognize more about this world, and love it even more. I am convinced that it is the creation of a loving God. Moreover, in many respects my experience of the world is consistent with what I have learned from decades of engagement with the Hebrew Scriptures. The Old Testament affirms the goodness of the world as God's creation and teaches its readers to love life. What the book of Deuteronomy recommends with regard to the effects of obedience to God can be generalized: "I have set before you life and death, blessings and curses. Choose life . . ." (Deuteronomy 30:19). However, this does not mean that all my childhood questions about the meaning of creation have been resolved.

The Old Testament on Aging

The basic attitude toward aging and the aged in the Old Testament seems quite straightforward, and on the surface relatively consistent. In ancient Israel, aging as such was not viewed as a crisis situation at all. To the contrary, age brought distinction, honor, and authority. The "elders" in effect ruled the society at the local level. Consistent with the commandment to honor one's father and mother was the view that those who are pious respect their elders. Thus the people are instructed: "You shall rise before the aged, and defer to the old; and you shall fear your God" (Leviticus 19:32). Just as children require particular care, the elderly are entitled to respect: It is a "grim-faced nation" that shows "no respect to the old or favor to the young" (Deuteronomy 28:50). To be sure, the very existence of these injunctions indicates that such respect for one's elders was by no means universal.

Clearly, to live to an old age was considered a blessing: Among God's promises to Abraham is that "you shall go to your ancestors in peace; you shall be buried in a good old age" (Genesis 15:15). The report of his death confirms the promise: "Abraham breathed his last and died in a good old age, an old man and full of years" (Genesis 25:8). This attitude to length of life seems almost universal: "You shall come to your grave in ripe old age, as a shock of grain comes up to the threshing floor in its season" (Job 5:26). Prophetic visions of salvation include the image of people living into old age:

> No more shall there be in [Jerusalem]
>   an infant that lives but a few days,
>   or an old person who does not live out a lifetime;
> for one who dies at a hundred years will be considered a youth,
>   and one who falls short of a hundred will be considered accursed.
> (Isaiah 65:20)

> Thus says the LORD of hosts: Old men and old women shall again sit in the streets of Jerusalem, each with staff in hand because of their great age.
> (Zechariah 8:4)

Certainly to die young was a curse: "See, a time is coming when I will cut off your strength and the strength of your ancestor's family, so that no one in your family will live to old age" (1 Samuel 2:31). To live, especially in the land that God gives (Deuteronomy 30:16), was a blessing; to die young was a tragedy and a curse.

But on the other hand, and when one looks more deeply, some ambivalence toward aging begins to surface. Clearly, ancient Israel knew full well that old age was not an unmixed blessing. One hardly finds a detailed account of aging, but there are frequent allusions to the limitations and the infirmities that come with advancing years. Many of the individual complaint psalms describe death—and with it life's final years—in effect as a process, with the gradual loss of mobility, light, and community. (See Psalms 6, 13, 22, 30, 38.[1]) Even Zechariah's prophecy of a Jerusalem filled with old men and women knows that the elderly will require staffs to get around.

In our time we can only imagine the difficulties brought on by aging eyes in the centuries before the invention of corrective lenses. More than once the Old Testament alludes to the problem: "Now the eyes of Israel were dim with age, and he could not see well" (Genesis 48:10). "Now Ahijah could not see, for his eyes were dim because of his age" (1 Kings 14:4).

Other physical problems, including being overweight, are associated with the elderly: "Eli fell over backward from his seat by the side of the gate; and his neck was broken and he died, for he was an old man, and heavy" (1 Samuel 4:18).

One of the more explicit comments about the limitations of aging is the poignant speech of King David's friend Barzillai, responding to the king's invitation to join him in Jerusalem: "Today I am eighty years old; can I discern what is pleasant and what is not? Can your servant taste what he eats or what he drinks? Can I still listen to the voice of singing men and singing women? Why then should your servant be an added burden to my lord the king?" (2 Samuel 19:35). Not only does he acknowledge that those who are old can become a "burden" to their family and friends, but his speech is prefaced with the acknowledgment of life's limitations: "How many years have I still to live, that I should go up with the king to Jerusalem?" (2 Samuel 19:34).

Sarah's laughter when God promises that she will bear a son clearly has to do with the fact that she is beyond childbearing age. But there is more: "After I have grown old, and my husband is old, shall I have pleasure?" (Genesis 18:12).

Even that magnificent account of Moses just before his death is a comment on the normal limitations of old age: "Moses was one hundred twenty years old when he died; his sight was unimpaired and his vigor had not abated" (Deuteronomy 34:7). If the lack of impairment were not so unusual—because there was no one like Moses—it would not have been noted. The leader's advanced age was no more miraculous than his good eyesight and his "vigor."

Responses to the World

Old Testament texts do not respond to the created order—what we call the natural world—with a single voice. Likewise, the Hebrew Scriptures express different attitudes toward the processes to which human beings are subject, including aging. The dominant perspective affirms the world as God's good creation, as in Genesis 1:31: "God saw everything that he had made, and indeed, it was very good." And numerous psalms praise God by describing the beauty of creation.

> The earth is the LORD's and all that is in it,
>   the world, and those who live in it;
> for he has founded it on the seas,
>   and established it on the rivers.
>   (Psalm 24:1-2)

> The heavens are telling the glory of God;
>   and the firmament proclaims his handiwork.
>   (Psalm 19:1)

But Koheleth—the author of the book of Ecclesiastes—looks at the same starry sky that evokes praise and wonder and is impressed with the repetitive cycles of nature:

> A generation goes, and a generation comes,
>   but the earth remains forever.
> The sun rises and the sun goes down,
>   and hurries to the place where it rises.
> The wind blows to the south,
>   and goes around to the north;
> round and round goes the wind,
>   and on its circuits the wind returns. (1:4-6)

Because there is nothing new under the sun, he is bored, depressed, or at most apathetic:

All things are wearisome;
　　more than one can express. . . .
What has been is what will be,
　　and what has been done is what will be done;
　　there is nothing new under the sun. (1:8-9)

As one looks more closely at the book as a whole, it becomes clearer that this attitude toward creation stems from Koheleth's frustration with human limits, especially old age and death. The book's final chapter presents a sad picture of the limitations of age and eventual death:

Remember your creator in the days of your youth, before the days of trouble come, and the years draw near when you will say, "I have no pleasure in them." (12:1)

Koheleth goes on to characterize aging and death,

before the silver cord is snapped, and the golden bowl is broken, . . . and the dust returns to the earth as it was, and the breath returns to God who gave it. (12:6-7)

But even Koheleth, who often sounds like a grumpy old man, cannot leave his readers without advice about facing and dealing with the natural processes that catch up all living things. In fact, the very act of reflecting upon the futility of life presumes that it is helpful to make sense of life and to transmit one's analysis and conclusions to others, including in writing. Like other wisdom writers, Koheleth attempts to make sense of life and the world, to bring all things into and under the purview of human thought. Even when these thinkers confront the limits of human understanding—Ecclesiastes and Job—they see value in presenting their reflections to others. Human life and the lives of individuals are viewed in the wider context of God's world as a whole.

Koheleth is resigned—almost stoic—in his attitude toward the world and human limits, but he has some recommendations for dealing with those boundaries: "Whoever is joined with all the living has hope, for a living dog is better than a dead lion" (9:4). And over and over he repeats: "There is nothing better for mortals than to eat and drink, and find enjoyment in their toil" (2:24). "Enjoy life with the wife whom you love, all the days of your vain life that are given you under the sun, because that is your portion in life . . ." (9:9).

It may be small comfort, but it is some comfort, to make the most of one's limited place in God's creation. Thus in view of the fact that all living things age, there is a tone of acceptance if not resignation in those most famous lines from Koheleth's book:

> For everything there is a season,
>   and a time for every matter under heaven:
> a time to be born, and a time to die;
> a time to plant, and a time to pluck up what is planted. . . . (3:1-2)

Psalm 104 offers a significantly different response to the natural world, and with it a very different attitude toward human limitations. In fact, if Ecclesiastes represents one extreme with its almost negative view of the natural order, then Psalm 104 stands at the other extreme. It expresses a joyful acceptance of the world as it is. Only in this Psalm and in Job 38–39, for example, do we find in the Hebrew Scriptures an unqualified appreciation of the wild as well as the domestic world.

Psalm 104 is a hymn of praise in which human beings address God, and their place in the natural order is treated explicitly.[2] This song, in some respects parallel to both Genesis 1 and Job 38–40, praises God as creator and sustainer of the world and all that dwell therein. It is remarkably sensual, filled with delightful sights and sounds, including the song of the birds. It mentions feelings of all kinds, especially pleasure: "The earth is satisfied with the fruit of your work" (v. 13), "to bring forth food from the earth, and wine to gladden the human heart" (vv. 14-15). There is a distinctly aesthetic dimension to creation, evoking pleasure in what one sees, hears, feels, and tastes.

Whereas in virtually all other Old Testament texts wild animals are feared, here (as in Job 38–39) they are admired and enjoyed. "The young lions roar for their prey, seeking their food from God" (v. 21). Even lions, the psalmist acknowledges, have to make a living. Both here and in Job, predators are shown taking care of their young, making it far more difficult to demonize the (potentially) dangerous animals.

This hymn takes in all living things and the divine gifts that sustain them, including water, food, shelter, and appropriate times. There is water for every wild animal (v. 11) and trees as habitat for the birds (v. 12). God causes "the grass to grow for the cattle"—that is, for domestic animals—and provides domestic "plants for people to use" (v. 14).

Human beings, as one species among all the others, are sustained by and enjoy the gifts of God (vv. 14-15, 26). In terms of neither the form nor the contents of this song are they singled out.[3] Similar to the content but not the tone of Ecclesiastes, all creatures have their times, marked by the sun and moon. The lions hunt at night, but retreat to their dens at sunrise, when people go out to work until evening (vv. 19-23). Moreover, when it looks to the sea (v. 26), the hymn expresses wonder both at the results of technology (ships) and the creatures beyond the bounds of culture (Leviathan).

Particularly relevant to reflection on aging, the limits of life are treated in a particularly matter-of-fact way (vv. 27-30). All living things depend on God for life, for their "food in due season." But when God's face is hidden they are dismayed: "when you take away their breath, they die." However, that is not the end, at least not for creation.

> When you send forth your spirit, they are created;
> and you renew the face of the ground. (v. 30)

Is this renewal, as usually understood, by means of the divine spirit, or—more literally—with the bodies of the dead? That is,

God renews the face of the ground with the dust that returns to dust. They are created out of the dust of the ground, and given life. In any case, the continuing cycle of renewal is a gift of God.[4] This is a sober and realistic acceptance of the world as it is, and the limits of life as faced by all human beings.

There are far worse responses to the natural world and to human limits than those in Ecclesiastes. Koheleth's reflections lead him to conclude that there is an appropriate time for all things, for age as well as youth, and that it is better to face and accept human limits than to deny them. But neither are Koheleth's the most helpful biblical words on these matters. The attitude of sad resignation reflects the limitations of preoccupation with oneself, and thus misses the persistent biblical concern with community and creation as a whole.

Psalm 104, on the other hand, like the divine speeches in Job 38–41, stresses that human beings are only a part—an essential part to be sure—of a vast and wonderful natural order, God's creation and design for all things. In attempting to make sense of life, these texts draw attention beyond the individual self and even the human species. Just as attention to history enables one to see one's place in the march of the generations, attention to the wonders of the world can locate one in the scheme of creation and the cycle of re-creation, all of which is in God's hands. The more one reflects upon and enjoys God's good world, the more one can accept and enjoy one's life—including all its stages—within that world.

Notes

1. This has been worked out in detail by Chr. Barth, *Die Errettung vom Tode in den individuellen Klage-und Donkliedern des Alten Testamentes* (1947).
2. The following discussion of Psalm 104 is adapted from Gene M. Tucker, "Rain on a Land Where No One Lives: The Hebrew Bible on the Environment," *Journal of Biblical Literature* 116 (1997), 3-17.
3. James L. Mays, *Psalms* (Interpretation; Louisville: John Knox Press, 1994), 334.
4. There is "a recognition of the absolute dependence of all creatures upon the LORD for food (vv. 27-30) and for life itself (vv. 29-30)." Mays, *Psalms*, 335.

10

⚜

RETIREMENT:
A WHOLE NEW LIFE

WILLIAM H. WILLIMON

Vanity of vanities, says the Teacher. . . .
All is vanity.
What do people gain from all the toil
at which they toil under the sun?
A generation goes, and a generation comes,
but the earth remains forever. . . .
There is nothing new under the sun.
—Ecclesiastes 1:2-4, 9

Then I saw a new heaven and a new earth; for the first heaven and the first earth had passed away. . . . And the one who was seated on the throne said, "See, I am making all things new."
—Revelation 21:1, 5

My text is from Ecclesiastes, one of the Bible's most depressing, cynical books. "Vanity of vanities, says the Teacher. . . . All is vanity." Have you ever felt like that, looking back on your life? Your accomplishments crumble in your hands as dust. Your great achievements seem as so much chasing after the wind.

No wonder the writer of Ecclesiastes feels this way about his life. "There is nothing new under the sun," he says. Life is just one thing after another, a great wheel in which there is no beginning and no end. Life is, in Shakespeare's words, full of "sound and fury, signifying nothing." Ecclesiastes is one of the only books in the Bible with a cyclical view of history. History doesn't begin or end; it's not going anywhere. History is a great cycle, a circle. There is nothing new under the sun. When there is no ending or beginning, no real newness, life is depressing.

The subject here is something that many of us will do, some sooner than later. The subject is retirement. I have a problem right from the start. When I preach, I like to preach from the Bible, take a biblical text and work from there. The trouble is, not until recently have humans lived long enough or had enough stored-up goods to "retire" in our sense of the word. The Bible, particularly the Hebrew Scripture, considers old age, a long life, a great gift of God. But the problem of retirement—what to do with our old age or our increasingly long life—is relatively recent.

The word *retirement* makes me very unhappy. It's a cousin of other similarly uninspiring words, such as *retreat, remove, regress. Retirement* makes it sound as if, in our last years of life, we withdraw from the fray, settle in, settle down, quit moving, and stop living for all intents and purposes. Yet we're learning that each stage of life, including retirement, has its challenges, its different demands and new adventures.

I recall a young man whom I was teaching in seminary. He was serving his first little church as a student pastor. One day he complained to me about his congregation. "The median age of my congregation is over sixty," he declared. "And you know how old people are." "How are they?" I asked. "You know—set in their ways, creatures of habit, slow to change, stuck in their ruts. They don't want any innovation or change in the way we do things at the church."

Not two days before, I had read an article on retirement that noted that, of the six or eight transitions we must make in life, the most traumatic changes—four or five of them—will occur after sixty-five. Radical moves like declining health, loss of independence, unemployment, and the loss of a spouse are among the major transitions of this stage of life.

I noted this to the young student pastor. "It's not fair to say that these older people are refusing to change. They are about to drown in some of the most dramatic changes life offers. When you've buried the man you have lived with for forty years, or you are forced out of your life's work, about the last thing you want is to come to church and have some upstart young preacher say, 'Let's do something new and innovative today.' They're sinking in a flood of innovation!"

We once thought of adulthood as that time in life when you at last put down roots, hunkered down, burrowed in for the rest of your life, and stayed there. The really important developmental events occurred in infancy, childhood, or youth. We now know that adulthood is best construed as a series of passages (thank you, Gail Sheehy), of life challenges, which are far from stable.

For some years I have taught a course to first-year students at Duke called "The Search for Meaning."[1] We study the ways various people have found meaning in their lives, a reason to get out of bed in the morning. We also push the students to articulate their own sense of meaning in life, to write down where they are headed and who they plan to be when they grow up. I have noted that most of them think to themselves, "I'm all confused and in flux now, but when I am twenty-five I will have decided who I want to be. I will settle down, settle in, and be fixed."

It doesn't take much insight to see that life is not at all like that. For instance, I note how odd it is for us to ask students, "What do you plan to do (or be) when you graduate from Duke?" They respond by saying, I'm going to be an electrical engineer." Or, "I'm going into medicine." But then we note that the average American goes through *seven* job changes in a lifetime. Someone from the Engineering School told me recently that they did a study of their graduates and only 30 percent of them were in engineering just twenty years after graduation!

See my point? These students had better be preparing for a more challenging life than merely deciding what they want to do and expecting to do that for the rest of their lives. Is that why increasing numbers of educators are coming to speak of intelligence not in terms of IQ, a fixed intellectual quotient with which you are born, but rather intelligence defined as *the ability to adapt?* Life is a long series of adaptations, moves, changes, beginnings and endings.

As a pastor, I've watched a good number of people move into retirement. I'm moving ever closer myself. And though, from what I've observed, there are a number of challenges of the alleged "Golden Years," one stands out above all the rest: Retirement is a whole new life.

I'm here paraphrasing from a great book by my friend Reynolds Price, *A Whole New Life.*[2] It's Reynolds's moving account of his struggle through cancer surgery, recovery, and beyond. What Reynolds has to say is far too rich to be condensed, but I think it fair to say that one of the most important insights of the book, and the insight that gives the book its title, is that he experienced his illness as an invitation to a whole new life.

Reynolds tells how he denied his cancer, how he was filled with anger and resentment when he realized that he was very sick, and how he struggled in the painful months after his debilitating but life-saving surgery. Here was a once robust, active man at the prime of his life, the peak of his career, reduced to life in a wheelchair.

But Reynolds depicts his path back as a dawning realization that, in his words, "the old Reynolds has died."[3] His old self, and so many of the aspects of his former existence that he loved, were over. He could not get them back. Now, he could spend the rest of his life in grief for what he had lost, pitifully attempting to salvage some bits and pieces, or he could begin "a whole new life."

Reynolds chose the latter. He began again. He started over. It was not the life he might have chosen, if he were doing the choosing, but it was a good life, a life worth living. He now enjoys the greatest period of artistic productivity of his life, turning out more novels, plays, and poems than ever. "Find your way to be somebody else," he advises, "the next viable you—a stripped-down whole other clear-eyed person, realistic as a sawed-off shotgun and thankful for air, not to speak of the human kindness you'll meet if you get normal luck."[4]

Now, retirement is rarely as traumatic as spinal cancer. Yet I do think there are analogies to be made. From what I've observed, the people who fail miserably at the challenges of the later years are those who fail to see retirement as a definite transition from one plane of existence to another. They attempt to salvage too much of their former life.

I'm haunted by what a woman told me of her mother. Her mother had worked at minimum wage in a garment factory for over forty years. When she retired, her children thought she would be thrilled. She was miserable. She cried. She hung around at the gate of the factory many mornings, vainly hoping that they would call her back to work. She even took an assumed name and tried to get hired, representing herself as another person.

That won't work. Your old life goes on without you. They somehow get by down at the office without your services. The school doesn't fall in after your last day in the classroom.

You can't get the old life back. You need to lay hold of a whole new life. I think those of us who are moving toward retirement could do much more to better prepare ourselves to make that transition to a whole new life. If our only life is our work, we are in big trouble unless we can find some new life after work. Churches could do a better job of helping members to prepare themselves and to support one another during the transition into retirement.

We need some good rituals for retirement. In Japan, for instance, there is a tradition in which, when a woman reaches retirement age, she takes all of her pots and pans and presents them to her daughter or daughter-in-law. From then on she is expected not to enter the kitchen. That part of her life is over. A new life has begun.

Many Japanese men begin retirement by dressing in a red kimono and doing something adventuresome that they have not done before, like climbing Mount Fuji. People need to be encouraged to do something visible and physical that will symbolize their important transition.

Thomas Naylor and I wrote a book entitled *The Search for Meaning* arising out of our first-year-student seminar. To our surprise and delight, a number of churches have reported using the book in congregational preretirement seminars. We're pleased that the book we wrote with college students in mind has proved to be helpful for those in their sixties. We are reminded that one of the most important skills one can have is the ability to take a deep breath, look out over one's life, and start over with a whole new life.

As Christians, we do not believe that history is a meaningless cycle going nowhere, one thing after another. We believe that God is Alpha and Omega, the Beginning and the End. God gives fresh beginnings, new days, new lives. The Bible opens with the Genesis declaration, "Let there be light!" as a new world comes into being, and closes, in Revelation, with "Behold, I make all things new!"

Between here and there, we are asked to make many transitions, each with attendant pain, uncertainty, and promise. One of the most important of our life transitions is retirement.

My father-in-law spent his entire life as a pastor in a variety of United Methodist churches in South Carolina. Mr. Parker had thus spent his adulthood in black suits and white shirts as moral exemplar of the community, doing his duty in the week-in-week-out care of his churches.

When he retired, he bought a large camping trailer, and he and Mrs. Parker pulled the trailer toward New England for a long-awaited retirement celebration trip. Somehow, on the way from South Carolina to New England, he took a wrong turn and found himself driving down the middle of Manhattan, pulling that trailer, lost, not knowing which way to turn.

A car blew its horn at him, pulled up beside him, and the driver shouted, "Old man, I wish you would figure out where you're going or get out of the way!" Mr. Parker said that he thought to himself, *I'm here in New York, a long way from South Carolina. Nobody here knows that I was a United Methodist preacher. I'm retired.* So he rolled down his window, looked over at the man in the car beside him, and said, "And I wish you would go to hell!"

Retirement. It's a whole new life.

Notes

1. Thomas Naylor and William H. Willimon, *The Search for Meaning* (Nashville: Abingdon Press, 1994).
2. Reynolds Price, *A Whole New Life: An Illness and a Healing* (New York: Atheneum, 1994).
3. Ibid., pp. 183 ff.
4. Ibid., p. 183.

11

⁂

POSITIVE SPINS ON
BAD IDEAS

⁂

ORLO C. STRUNK, JR.

I'm going to take it as axiomatic that the processes of growing old and of dying are bad ideas and that all of us, if we had our druthers, would like to live forever. Of course, such an axiom assumes a few conditions—that we would be in relatively good health, that we would remain thirty-nine years old until the universe runs down, and that we would know at thirty-nine everything we know in these twilight years of life.

Equally axiomatic, I wager, is the presence of idiosyncratic factors; that is, that people's preferences in this regard probably vary extensively. For instance, I am fairly sure that there are those who would not choose thirty-nine as the ideal frozen year, or that they might disagree over what constitutes "relatively good health." And knowing that some people, by dint of their temperament, find essential glee in disagreeing with any generalization, there will be those who claim that growing old is a gentle and meritorious process to be savored and celebrated. There might even be those who, through the web of temperament, personality, genetic programming, social standing, faith commitments, and such, would consider death just another phase of life—a phase to be cherished and considered a sort of adventure akin to floating down the Amazon or diving for pearls in the blue waters of the South Pacific.

Still, I remain convinced that most of us value radical longevity and the sort of functional wisdom and good health that make for pleasure and a sense of well-being.

If, then, growing old and dying are indeed bad ideas, as I am claiming, what kind of *spin*—as they say in the contemporary political arena—can one put on these seemingly inevitable processes? It's not easy, I can tell you—or it's not easy without slipping into the bog of denial. In this regard, I recall a bishop of my church at a dinner party observing his seventy-first birthday, spending nearly an hour trying to convince us that "life really begins at seventy-one!" As I listened to the good ecclesiastic (I think I was about forty years old at the time), I found myself doubting his words, despite their elegance and the fact that he was, after all, a bishop. I didn't believe him then, and now that I'm his age, I don't believe him today. Nor am I impressed when I hear other less authoritative personages claim, one way or another, that being old is somehow a wonderful state of affairs (putting aside the oft-quoted retort that the alternative is even worse).

I must admit that this skepticism of mine causes me not a little consternation, even at times a smattering of self-doubt, even periods of guilt. I mean, after all, I could be wrong. Perhaps it is just me—maybe all this has to do with my failure at "growing old gracefully," as they say.

At any rate, I'm feeling that growing old is not, as Maurice Goudeket's charming book implies, a delight—although I must admit Goudeket almost had me convinced. Indeed, he did challenge me to work hard at *spin*. Early on in his essay, for instance, he flings at the reader this gauntlet:

And you, the seventy-five-year-olds, instead of helping to spread the usual mistaken notion based on mere superficial appearances, as you usually do, you ought to look into your hearts: apart from growing purer and more refined, has the "me" of your first adult years changed in any way? There is shortness of breath, a slowness of movement, a back that will not bend so easily, to be sure, but these are things for our bodies to cope with. The immaterial being that gives our threatened building all its life does not show a single wrinkle, nor will it ever do so.[1]

He is quite right, particularly if one is inclined to join him in his metaphysical assumption that soul and body are at the very least acquaintances if not codependents.

Nevertheless, I do find myself agreeing that old age has a way of generating a greater sensitivity of soul. And too—at least on most days—I am absolutely amazed at how, *internally,* I remain thirty-nine or thereabouts. It is a strange phenomenon, this sense that I haven't really changed that much since my "first adult years."

Lately, I have come to appreciate several condiments that in previous years I did not appear to have tasted, at least not in their full measure.

For one thing, I find that I now enjoy reading in a way peculiarly different from what I experienced in younger days. Although I cannot recall a time in my life when I did not enjoy reading, I now realize that much of it was adjunctive to my soul. By this I mean that except for the childhood comic books and the adolescent pulp magazines—all of which I read with abandon—much adult reading was a secondary activity tied to forms of accomplishments and advancements, usually in the educational arena. In the academy, where I spent most of my adult life, one often reads to keep up with ambitious graduate students or to gain advancement in professorial rank or to achieve tenure or simply to enhance one's professional performance and stature. Much of that kind of reading carries a forced-feeding quality to it, certainly not the savor of a true gourmet.

Another new propensity I have noticed of late is that I enjoy good writing more than the particular content of the writer's aims. It is the form and the style that provide me with unusual pleasure; the content seems quite a weak secondary reward.

This same sort of sensitivity seems evident as well in the simple act of seeing or observing. This is a peculiar and somewhat ironic development—for the physical fact is that my eyesight is nowhere near what it was in younger times. The fact is—and it comes to me as a frightful fact—that on my most recent visit to the optician I was informed that in two or three years I could expect to stand in need of cataract surgery. That she made this announcement in a perfunctory fashion did not soften my response to her prophecy. It was, and remains, a dreadful development, only one of old age's more nasty blows. At the same time—and this is the ironic dimension of it all—I experience a clarity of vision of the environment not previously evident. The smallest object now catches my attention—a tiny pollywog in our water garden, a Carolina wren resting far back in the crook of a pine tree, a baby chameleon clinging to a cattail.

This relatively new sight appears to spill over into my literary interests and preferences as well. It is illustrated by my growing attraction to *haiku*, an ancient Japanese poetic form that manages, sometimes with breathtaking strokes, to reward the reader with a single impression of a natural phenomenon—a phenomenon that those of us less sensitive to our surroundings frequently pass by. The form has led even me to "see" in ways previously overlooked.

> The crows take their stand,
> black figures deep in the woods—
> waiting like old age.

I find too that aging has softened both my anger and my impatience over things that don't go my way. A perfectionistic tendency has always plagued my soul. As a colleague once remarked to me, "It is difficult to be perfect in such an imperfect world." I have learned, too slowly, that it is not only difficult, it is impossible and frustrating. As a result, often I have harbored a deep and pervasive anger—anger at myself as well as at a world that did not behave as I would want. And anger spawned from that particular cauldron—a mixture of impossibilities and frustrations—leads almost certainly to a toxin as deadly as any emitted by the most greedy and irresponsible of industrial nations.

In that sense, the aging process seems to act as something of a prophylactic against the emotion of anger. I say this in the realization that I may be applying a level of wisdom to this that reaches considerably beyond the actual realities of this developmental phase. In fact, it may be, as the young critics frequently claim, that slowness to anger is merely the natural result of loss of élan, the degeneration of the life force, the slow demise of spirit. I am perfectly willing to consider such interpretations; nevertheless, the argument does not dim the actual joy and peace that come from robbing anger of its destructive force.

Finally, I appear to be at the period in my life when I unashamedly engage in drawing on my memory, in reflecting on my past, and even in ruminating over the events and processes of my life. To some, especially the young, this propensity may be judged as the manifestation of senility, an irritant to those whose past may be short and relatively uneventful. Although I can understand such an attitude—and in fact I myself have been bored by an older person reciting past experiences—I nevertheless find a peculiar joy in recollecting persons and events of my younger times. And with this backward look has come a kind of awe over how well I can accomplish this feat. That is, I am struck by the extent and detail of these mental exercises.

Recently, as an example, I undertook the task of recalling and describing in detail the layout of the house in which I was born. Although sixty years have passed since I lived in that structure, I found that with only a moderate amount of mental strain I could visualize every part of that home, from its cellar to its attic. Once more, I could feel a bit of the aura, or the numinous, if you will, associated with the place, a place in which early developments and transitions were negotiated.

It causes me little concern that others may find such recollections boresome or pathetic. At this period of life, the recalled events remain invigorating and pleasurable, and indeed they add a note of the providential to contemporary living.

Now the discerning reader will find little in this essay that addresses the topic of death. I suspect that particular blind spot can partly be explained by a simple and direct admission—I am only just beginning to contemplate that reality. Not having experienced death, I feel less than an amateur on the topic. Yes, of course, I have done the required reading—the denial of death, how we die, my faith's promises, and so forth. And my calling has had me counseling with grieving survivors, and I have seen death close up in a variety of settings. But I have not experienced it.

My hunch is, given the nature of some of the characteristics I have noted relative to growing old, death too probably will have some surprising qualities about it. Beyond that, at this particular point in life death remains a rather bad idea.

Note

1. Maurice Goudeket, *The Delights of Growing Old* (Pleasantville, N.Y.: The Akadine Press, 1996), p. 3.

12

.ᗢ.

IT'S A SWEET LIFE

ᗢ

KATHLEEN NORRIS

*Old monks are wild as well as simple. They perch more lightly
on the globe than the rest of us.*

—Peter Levi, *The Frontiers of Paradise*

While monasteries are renowned for their sacred spaces, the imposing churches and cloister walks that speak eloquently of silence, their holiest places are often not silent at all, but resound with conversation. In the "retirement center," "care center," or "hospital wing"—pick your euphemism—where many of the oldest members of a community reside, the oral history of the monastery is most alive. Such places in the outside world are commonly called "nursing homes," and are much dreaded. Monasteries cannot help reflecting their culture, and Benedictines are not immune from the fear of old age and lack of respect for the elderly that mar American society. Community life, as Benedictines practice it, is so intense that over the years a perceived slight or the abuse of power can become heavy baggage; thus you sometimes find middle-aged monks who feel they have a score to settle with an older monk, who years ago may have been their teacher, boss, formation director, or abbot. But when community works as it should, its elderly have the self-respect of people who have spent a lifetime listening and being listened to.

Monasteries also demonstrate, often in surprising ways, that when several generations of people are living together, the place of the very old is to teach about possibility. The monk or sister who can speak of planting the venerable trees in the cloistered garden or of building the stone fence that marks off the monastery enclosure may prove inspiring to a newcomer who feels stuck in the tedious, unglamorous tasks of the novitiate: cleaning and waxing floors, washing windows, working in the compost pile and flower beds, wondering what all of this has to do with a life dedicated to God.

The monastic retirement center is a place where one often encounters old people in whom pretense has been so stripped away that their holiness is palpable. Turn the lights off and you suspect that they might begin to glow in the dark, radiating the "openness to all" and transparency of heart that scholar Peter Brown tells us made Anthony of the Desert recognizable to fourth-century pilgrims even in a crowd of black-robed monks. The novices assigned to care for the aged and infirm members of a community frequently discover that this sort of holiness is most evident in people who have endured with patience and grace many years of debilitating illness and prolonged physical pain. This is not at all a romanticizing of illness but a recognition that people can sometimes transform physical sickness into health of soul. The example of a sister who is a calm, centered, quietly joyful and generous person, and who has suffered for years from a degenerative neurological disease, means more to a young nun than any book of theology or class on monastic history. In her own community she's found a woman who helps her to put many great souls of the Christian tradition into perspective: Hildegard, Julian of Norwich, Thérèse of Lisieux, all of whom converted their physical suffering into a love so profound that we are still reaping the benefits.

The stereotypical monk has a faith that is serene and certain. The reality is otherwise, especially for younger monastics, who often struggle mightily with issues of faith and belief. Near the end of a recent Monastic Institute, a week full of illuminating talks by a contemplative French Benedictine, Ghislain Lafont, an anguished young Trappist spoke up: "We've spoken of the loss of faith in American society. But what of loss of faith within the monastery itself?" He indicated that he was living, as a monk, with profound doubts, and that while the monastery was where he felt he belonged, at times his life there was nearly unbearable. Fr. Lafont nodded; none of this, evidently, was a surprise to him. What he said in response struck me as both practical and thoroughly monastic: "Of course we are weak, unable to cope. But if we can maintain faith, hope, and charity, it will radiate somehow. And people who come to us may find in us what we can no longer see in ourselves."

If Benedictine life is about loving others, about seeking God within the human community, then the means of salvation is at hand, right there in the other monks. Both those who offer love and support, and those who are incompatible or unsympathetic, can teach the young monastic what it means to incarnate Christ, to become the sort of person who radiates love. In this context, friendships within the monastery can become an inspiration to all. Over lunch one day with several Benedictine sisters, I was treated to stories of two nuns, long-deceased, who had become inseparable as they aged. One of the women had lost most of her hair and had taken to wearing a bright red wig. One morning the wig was even more askew than usual, but as the two walked arm in arm into chapel for lauds, her friend was overheard to say to her, "My, you look lovely this morning." When one of the women had to enter the convent nursing home and leave her friend behind, she said to her, "Don't forget about me." And her friend replied, "How could I forget you? You're my better self."

Younger monastic people revel in such stories, such lives. They may never have known their own grandparents well, but they come to feel, in the monastery, that they've found many grandparents, guides to life within the community, exemplars for the arduous journey. The living-out of vows is not respected in America. Our commitments are disposable, and if a marriage, or life in a monastic community, isn't working out, we tend to move on. And young monks and nuns can't help but suffer from the tension; committed as they are, they retain an edge, a tension that only time in the monastery can wear away. But when younger monastics, still attuned to the competitive values of the world, are delegated to care for older ones, the dimensions of commitment become clearer. As they steer a recalcitrant older sister toward the bathroom, or the chapel, an inner voice reminds them. *This is what you can hope to become.*

It's a message that can transform them. Young monks pray with sick old men whose piety seems terribly out of date, only to discover that as monks they have more in common than not. Listening well, they can hear the things that will help make them monks. "On Candlemas one year," a young monk told me, "I was overwhelmed to hear a brother say that as he grew older, he'd become more content to be like Simeon, an old man who spends his time sitting in the temple and waiting for the promised savior."

I once said to a good friend, a monk in his thirties, that while I loved him very much, it was the guys who'd been in the monastery for fifty years or more who really appealed to me. He sighed, and said, "This life is like being in a rock tumbler, which is really great, if you want to come out good and polished." It's not a bad comparison. Older monks and nuns often do attain an enduring and radical beauty, the many years of discipline having uncovered a freedom that others find inviting. While they usually have no certification as "spiritual directors," something of a craze these days among younger monastics, these elderly are often the ones people turn to. Although they are genuinely humble and would refuse the designation, they have a wisdom and holiness that others recognize and draw from. Encountering them can be a dazzlement, a revelation of holy simplicity.

At the end of the Monastic Institute one year I paid a visit to one of my favorite people in the world, an elderly monk who is going blind. He is going blind as he has lived, with feistiness and grace, and without losing gratitude for the many blessings of a long life. As always, he apologized for his messy room, and then he proudly showed off his latest accoutrement: a tape recorder on which he listens to the current issue of *America,* and also the latest books on the liturgical theology that has been his life's work.

He asked if I would come with him to call on another monk who had taken a bad fall the day before. This was a monk I'd not met, a priest who had only recently retired, in his mid-eighties, from many years of serving as a chaplain in a prison not far from the monastery. Other monks had spoken of this man with admiration, as someone who was humbly realistic about his ministry. "He knew that a lot of the prisoners came to Mass for something to do, just to get out of their cell," one young monk had told me, adding, "and that was enough for him. He just kept at it, hoping to do some good."

The nurse was leaving his room. She told us he'd been napping off and on all morning, awaiting transport to a nearby hospital for a CAT scan. He'd hit his head in the fall and the doctors needed to know the extent of his injuries. I was nervous about disturbing a man who might be sleeping or in great pain, not wanting company. Nothing could have prepared me for what happened. Another nurse entered the room and called out, "You have a visitor. Two visitors." We heard a weak voice respond, "Ah . . . it's a sweet life." As we entered the room, and he got a look at us, he said again, "It's a sweet life."

Gregory the Great tells a story in his *Dialogues* about a man who visited St. Benedict in his hermitage, explaining that as it is Easter he has brought a gift of food. Benedict says to him, "I know that it is Easter, for I have been granted the blessing of seeing you." Standing in that monastery nursing home, I felt that I'd just been blessed in the same earth-shaking way. The monk's greeting was the epitome of Benedictine hospitality—in his Rule Benedict says simply, "All guests who present themselves are to be welcomed as Christ"— and it also brought home to me the incarnational nature of monasticism. It is not a theory or even a theology, but a way of life.

All week at the Institute we had pondered and discussed the fundamentals of "the monastic way," such essentials as sacred reading, liturgy, work, silence, vigilance, and stability. Now, in the presence of two elderly monks with well over a century of lived monastic experience between them, the point of all this was made clear: to so form people in community, stability, and hospitality that they can welcome each other, and life itself, as sweet, despite the savage ups and downs, despite the indignities of old age and physical infirmity.

The elderly monk in that hospital bed would probably be startled to hear how beautiful he was to me as he lay there with a hideously bruised face; how he radiated the love of Christ; how I felt as if a desert *abba* had given me words I didn't even know I needed— *"It's a sweet life."* I don't know what he was like as a young man, but I'm sure he struggled, like every other Benedictine I've known, to become a monastic person. He'd probably hasten to assure me that he struggles still, that he is still in need of spiritual guidance and correction in pursuing "conversion of heart," a vow unique to the Benedictines. Yet with one simple gesture, he had powerfully demonstrated to me the incarnational nature of Christian faith, how, to paraphrase Teresa of Avila, we are the only eyes, mouth, hands, feet, and heart that Christ has on earth.

He was an ill, old man, and not one but two people had come to see him. What could it be but sweetness, and God's blessing? His welcome refreshed me and made me see something that's easy to lose sight of in our infernally busy lives. That we exist for each other, and when we're at a low ebb, sometimes just to see the goodness radiating from another can be all we need in order to rediscover it in ourselves.